The Theatre Student

ACTING

The Theatre Student

ACTING

Ruth Rawson

PUBLISHED BY
RICHARDS ROSEN PRESS, INC.
NEW YORK, N.Y. 10010

Standard Book Number 8239–0150–5
Library of Congress Catalog Card Number: 68–21664
Dewey Decimal Classification: 792

Published in 1970 by Richards Rosen Press, Inc.
29 East 21st Street, New York City, N. Y. 10010

First Edition

Manufactured in the United States of America

For the four: Al and Bertha, Paul, Tom.

RUTH RAWSON received the B.A. degree at Cornell College, M.F.A. at the Yale Drama School, and is currently completing the doctoral program at Columbia University. Her directing credits include seven seasons in professional summer theatres and direction of the Obie Award-winning *Comic Strip,* as well as *Kiss Mama* for Off-Broadway and *Poker Game* for Broadway. She has directed television productions for Omnibus and CBS. Mrs. Rawson has directed such major performers as Orson Bean, Walter Matthau, Martha Scott, Mildred Dunnock, Dennis King, Phyllis Newman, Tammy Grimes, William Daniels, and Martin Balsam. She is an instructor in the Speech and Theatre Arts department of St. John's University, teaches Oral Interpretation at Teachers College, Columbia University, and in the summer session of the Neighborhood Playhouse Theatre School. She has performed on radio and television, acting as hostess on a weekly half-hour interview show on WPIX. She has played leading roles in stock and showcase productions and makes solo appearances for women's clubs and drama groups. Mrs. Rawson is a member of the Speech Association of America, Speech Association of the Eastern States, American Educational Theatre Association, and Phi Beta Kappa.

Acknowledgments

Drawings by Donald P. Creason

SPECIAL PERMISSIONS

"Stopping by Woods on a Snowy Evening," from *Complete Poems of Robert Frost*. Copyright 1923 by Holt, Rinehart & Winston, Inc. Copyright 1951 by Robert Frost. Reprinted by permission of the publishers.

Angel Street by Patrick Hamilton. Constable & Company, Ltd., London, publishers. Reprinted by permission of the Hamilton estate.

"Four Little Foxes" from *Covenant with Earth: a Selection from the Poems of Lew Sarett*. Edited and copyright 1956 by Alma Johnson Sarett. University of Florida Press. Reprinted by permission of Mrs. Sarett.

"Do Not Go Gentle into That Good Night" from *Collected Poems* by Dylan Thomas. Copyright 1952 by New Directions Publishing Corporation. Reprinted by permission of the publishers.

I Remember Mama by John Van Druten. Harcourt, Brace & World, Inc., New York. Reprinted by permission of the publishers.

Preface

Ruth Rawson's biography convinces us that she knows what acting is all about. It takes a special talent to break down the course of its attainment, to make the student see that the "actor" does not spring "full blown from the head of Zeus," but that he can and must learn the techniques of the craft and happily become an actor and perhaps an artist.

Ruth Rawson has laid down paths for the actor, explicitly, professionally, and never pedantically or dully. I read and read and was intrigued all over again and wanted to become an actor.

Mildred Dunnock

FOREWORD

If you have talent, this book will help
you develop it. If you have no talent, this
book will do nothing for you except give you
many hours of pleasurable reading.

WALTER MATTHAU

Introduction

The overall growth in the number of amateur theatre groups, and the wide extension, in both number and complexity, of theatre presentations in high schools, colleges, and community groups gives evidence that the "participating theatre" is filling important needs. Of major importance, surely, is the providing of a channel for some of the demands and talents of young people and offering opportunities for enjoyment and benefit to adults whose main occupation lies in other fields. Assuming the thoughts and experiences of a character apart from one's own self, communicating, through that character, with others on the stage, and finally enlarging that communication to encompass an audience provide the three elements that John Gielgud says are inherent in acting—escape, pleasure, and responsibility.

The business of acting has always had about it an aura of glamour and excitement that is part of the "escape" and "pleasure." This book is an endeavor to help the beginning actor fulfill the demands that must be met in order to achieve that pleasure. It is the largest of the three elements—the responsibilities of preparing the part.

Contents

The Theatre Student

ACTING

Chapter I

READ THE PLAY AND
CHOOSE A PART

Let's take up a matter of wording first—the use of the term "amateur." It is often used in an erroneous sense as synonymous with inferior or inept or unfinished. The word "amateurs" in theatrical language simply means people not earning a living as actors, as opposed to "professionals"—people for whom acting is a means of earning a livelihood, and there it ends. I have seen and directed some amateur productions that were far more effective than many professional performances. The term "amateur" is not, then, an adjective denoting inability. For the period of time that you are playing any specific part you are an actor. Not "amateur" or "professional"—just "good" or "bad."

From your own experience in seeing plays and movies or watching television dramas, you know how widely types of roles and styles of acting vary. There's a long step from the gun-totin' hombre in a Western to Mildred Dunnock in *Death of a Salesman*, but they're both acting, and each has its place.

Your own particular style of acting will be as individual as your fingerprints—similar to many others, but never exactly the same, first because you *are* an individual, and second because acting is not a precise study. In math you can get one right answer; and anything else is wrong. In tennis you must master the correct way of hitting a ball and do it consistently, or you don't score. No such rigid methods and principles underlie the development of acting ability, but neither is good acting a matter of being divinely right just because an actor "feels it that way." So we'll examine the business of acting in as precise a way as we can, studying the tools and instruments the actor must develop and use and the structure that goes into the difficult and fascinating creation known as acting.

If you know now of a part you will be playing, or if tryouts are coming up and there's a part you hope to get, step one is to acquire a copy of the script—your own, so that you may mark it up any way you want to. If you don't have a play or a part in mind, go to the script of *Lawyer Lincoln*, which is printed in the back of the companion volume *Directing* by Dr. Paul Kozelka and get three or four other people to undertake their role preparation along with you so you can do scenes, if not the whole play.

Your first project (described again in the Work Assignments at the end of the chapter) will be to read the play just for the story and entertainment of it. At the end of this first reading you will write down some notes of reaction to it, such as which scenes stand out in a special way, what surprises were found either in plot development or within characters, which sequences seemed too long, which characters were clearly defined, which seemed vague. You will then have done something that you can never do again, and that is to react to the play with the total spontaneity of first acquaintance. Once you've read the script and know what happens, you are launched on the long road of mastering the difficult techniques that will build in you the ability to listen and react each time as if it were the first time you had ever been with these particular people at this particular moment and heard that particular line.

The play and part you have chosen as your basis for study may be one already well known, or one you have seen on the stage or in motion pictures or television. Your job, still, will be to approach the part as nearly as possible as if you had never seen it, and to find the reality of your character through your own work. It is never satisfactory to try and copy another actor's performance, because even the best imitation is still just that—an exterior set of trappings without any truth at its core. Certainly, however, most roles have certain basic characteristics that an actor may not change without destroying the part or altering the author's intent. To take off on a radical new approach just for the sake of being different is just as false as slavish imitation. Because each production of a play is greatly influenced by the concept of the director, by the casting, and by the design of the production, it often happens that *reading* a play may spark in you a quite different idea of the whole thing than the one you saw performed. And as you begin work and continue the developing of your character you will be constantly trying and discarding, testing and refining each new idea that presents itself. New part or old, you will be striving to arrive at the reality of your character.

A tremendous surge has taken place in the popularity of musicals for school and community groups, based at the outset, no doubt, on the stunning success of the musical in commercial theatre and on television. As amateur groups gradually ceased to be overawed by the immensity of the production and decided to take a try at *South Pacific* or *West Side Story* or *My Fair Lady,* they found that the musical, although presenting some special problems, has success built in. Success, at least in terms of audience reaction, can be guaranteed. And the particular exhilaration in doing a musical lies in the diversity of talents that may be utilized—actors, singers, dancers, musicians, costumers, scene painters, lighting enthusiasts, carpenters—*everybody* works on a musical!

From your standpoint as an actor, the approach to your character and the major problems and challenges in its building are the same as those of a straight play, so proceed on that basis if you've chosen a role in a musical for your study. Later chapters will discuss some differences of technique that are required for the speaking areas of musicals as well as the songs, and also for playing them in what is called "the round," or "arena" style.

It would be great if just reading a book about acting produced some sort of automatic absorption, like osmosis, that simply effected the desired results without any mental or physical exertion on the part of the student. Well, you know it doesn't happen that way any more than you can learn to play the piano by looking at it, or reading books about it, or listening to other people play. You must think of this beginning study of acting as an actual work project. Each chapter will list these projects specifically, up to the point of going into rehearsal. Many of them should be continued throughout the entire rehearsal period; some will be related to only a certain area of the study of your part, but whatever the directions are, follow them carefully and faithfully. Be your own critic and instructor in judging which work assignments you need to continue doing.

The training of your voice, body, mind, and imagination for acting will produce rewards in every area of personal, school, and community activity. Acting is, after all, a part of the whole business of communication, and that's what you spend the major portion of your life doing—communicating with others.

WORK ASSIGNMENTS

1. Get a copy of the play you wish to use as the basis for study. It is essential that you apply the assignments to a specific role in either a play or a musical and that you own a copy so that you may make notations in it. If you have no specific play in mind, use the script of the one-act play *Lawyer Lincoln* by Betty Smith and Chase Webb, which is printed in the back of the book *The Theatre Student: Directing*.

2. Read the play from beginning to end at *one sitting*. Don't read a few pages or an act and then pick it up later. If your read-ing is interrupted, start again at the beginning so that you do it in one continuous reading.

3. Make the notes suggested earlier in this chapter and any other notations of first impressions about the play that occur to you. Don't write these in the book, but keep them on a separate sheet of paper for later reference.

4. If a play, either amateur or professional, is showing somewhere in your area, go to see it. If you can't do this, go to see a "straight" movie or watch a television production of a play. By "straight" is meant something other than a musical or a production that is wildly offbeat. Historical movies often provide excellent character studies in a wide variety of age level. Decide on one actor whose performance you wish to watch specifically. After the performance, write a brief assessment of the whole play and then of your character in particular. Was he real and convincing? Did he *listen?*

A scene from Shakespeare's Romeo *and* Juliet, *staged at the University of Redlands, Redlands, Calif. Directed by Albert and Bertha Johnson.*

Chapter II

PRODUCING THE VOICE

Now let us look specifically at the responsibilities of the actor as we begin the preparation for playing a role. What are these responsibilities?

First to come to mind, probably, is the ability to speak so that one can be heard and understood. When anything is so clearly vital to a successful performance it is hard to understand why so many performers fail this primary step. Everything else is dependent upon it. You may be able to move beautifully and meaningfully about the stage, you may have developed a psychological background and understanding for your character that is creative and true, but if you can't be heard past the first three rows you might as well go home and forget the whole thing.

The miracle of speech is certainly one of our least understood and most taken-for-granted blessings. Since it is a nearly universal talent, unlike being a musician or a gifted artist or an outstanding athlete, it is assumed that to be able to talk, just as you do now, is quite sufficient—that speech is a talent that needs no training. Not so.

Do you know what is meant by "diaphragm breathing"? A large muscle called the diaphragm separates the chest cavity from the abdominal cavity. It is attached to the ribs, and the rib cage provides the means for knowing whether you are breathing diaphragmatically. A still-dominant misconception is that taking a deep breath is properly accompanied by a violent hunching upwards of the shoulders. Nothing could be further from the case. In proper breathing of all kinds—whether it be the "quiet breathing" you are doing now as you read silently, breathing for phonation, which you do when you speak, or so-called "deep breathing" for anything from blowing up a balloon to playing a trumpet, expansion is evident in the lower rib cage, and the shoulders do not move upward.

For some reason, or for several reasons, if you have studied diaphragm breathing for singing, this does not guarantee that you are using it when you speak. The singer depends on taking in a large amount of air, gaining maximum expansion, and then using it in a way that will make it last through entire phrases, which are almost always a great deal longer than the phrases we use in speaking. For instance, if you were to recite in an auditorium (hence having to project to be heard) the first lines of *America,* you might take a catch breath after "My country, 'tis of thee" and again after "Sweet land of liberty" before completing the thought with "Of thee I sing." If you were singing it in the same circumstances, the chances are you would eliminate the first or maybe both pauses for breath. The playing of Shakespeare, Shaw, and some of the classics requires that the actor be able to support very long phrasing, but in most cases the actor should be a spendthrift with his breath and use it freely to support a full, relaxed, projected voice. In both singing and speaking, however, the use of diaphragm breathing permits us to vary the rate and force of expiration (breathing out) without using throat tension.

The specific set of exercises at the end of the chapter should be done for only one or two minutes at a time, many times per day, faithfully and precisely. This is imperative. If you follow the directions, it should be a matter of only a few weeks before diaphragm breathing has become completely automatic, and you have all the expansion you will ever need. I don't swear to all the fringe benefits that some enthusiasts claim for this form of breathing, such as a noticeable reduction of colds and other respiratory ailments, but you will begin to notice very soon a deepening of pitch and enriching of your vocal quality. This is the first of the noticeable results and there are no tricks to it. It works.

The daily exercises are designed so that you can check your progress. When you can do the twelfth day of the Christmas sequence all on one breath, that's the longest you could conceivably *need* to talk on one breath.

Most important is that you start working for a little expansion, gradually increase it, and by diligent practice make it your natural method of breathing. It *is* the natural way because it is the manner in which we start breathing from birth, but somewhere along the way upper chest breathing gets substituted in most people, and diaphragm breathing has to be relearned. It is the first step in starting your preparation; mastering it will enable you to accomplish with a minimum of tension and a maximum of effectiveness the two demands that differentiate breathing for speech from quiet breathing, i.e., the air must be expelled with greater force, and the exhalation period is controlled and is much longer than the inhalation period.

It isn't necessary that you have detailed knowledge of the vocal mechanism, but since it is one of your four major tools, you should know how it operates. The windpipe, otherwise known as the trachea, is literally that. It is the tube through which the air is expelled by your breathing out, blowing the vocal bands apart and making them flutter to produce the basic sound from which you will mold every peep, squeak, word, note, roar, or growl you ever utter.

The vocal bands, which stretch across the top of the windpipe, are small, varying in length from a little over half an inch in women up to about one inch in men, and the length and thickness of them are two determiners of the basic pitch level of your voice. Just as the heaviest string on a violin, guitar, or any stringed instrument is always the deepest in pitch, similarly the longer and thicker the vocal cords, the deeper the pitch of the voice. The third factor in determining the pitch is the amount of tension. When you wish to tune a guitar string upwards you turn the peg to increase the tension, and vocally the same rising of pitch occurs when we are under some particular tension such as excitement or fear. This also explains why the pitch of the voice often becomes deeper when one begins to use diaphragm breathing, since throat and vocal tension is being reduced.

In quiet breathing, which you are doing now if you are reading silently, these small vocal bands, which are actually the edges of two membranes attached to the rim of the trachea, are in a V formation, together at the front of the trachea and wide apart at the back. The exhaled air passes through this open space without sound since there is nothing blocking its way.

When you decide to say something, you don't go through any conscious preparation. You don't say to yourself, "Now I'm going to fix my vocal bands so I can speak." What happens is that the impulse to speak is transmitted by the brain to the proper nerves and muscles so that the vocal bands snap into a closed position—the V is closed and they are touching each other from front to back. *Now* the air, in order to get through, must blow them apart, causing them to vibrate and produce sound.

If you constructed a model of the vocal mechanism to approximate this basic sound you would hear a rather lifeless hollow "blat." Everything that changes this basic sound into the forty-four or more different sounds we have in the English language, and into all the ranges of pitch, loudness, quality, and length of sounds, is done by *you* by means of resonators and articulators.

Some of these work for you without your doing anything about it. For instance, you can feel the resonating in your upper chest and in your larynx if you will place one hand on your chest, the other against the front of your throat, and say in a good full voice, "Oh, what a beautiful morning!" Other spaces are also working for you as resonators without conscious effort or control on your part. But three major contributors to resonance are controlled by you, and they are the oral cavity, the throat cavity (pharynx), and the nasal passages.

Try this simple experiment. Make a sustained sound of "ooh" and after you hold it for a count of three, change quickly to the *broadest* ear-to-ear smile that you can possibly manage—still continuing to make a vocal sound. Now start again with the sustained "ooh," go to the smile, then open your mouth as *wide* as you can—still continuing to make a vocal sound. Whether or not you intend to, you see that you went from "ooh" to "eee" to "aah," by changing the size and shape of the *oral cavity*. This is the resonating cavity that we can most consciously and effectively control, and in most of our everyday speech it is badly neglected. Most people just plain don't open their mouths wide enough to produce properly resonated sounds.

You will be aware of changing the size and shape of the *throat cavity* if you first say "aah" and then go to the short "a" sound as in "cat." Say just the two vowel sounds, al-

ternating from one to the other several times. Notice that you are making very little difference in how wide you open your mouth, but what can you feel happening with your tongue? Because the center and back parts of your tongue are rising for the short "a" sound, you have changed the size and shape of the throat cavity and hence produced a sound other than "aah."

As you see, we've been using vowel sounds for these demonstrations of resonance. All of the vowel sounds are voiced and are capable of being sustained and reinforced by resonance. Most consonants are some form of stopping sound and so are not concerned in any major way with resonance. However, one small and very important group of consonants capable of being sustained is the nasal group, and they are dependent on resonance through the *nasal passages* for their distinctive sounds. If you say the word "naming" you have used every nasal sound in the English language—m, n, and ng. These are the *only* nasal sounds, and if your own voice is sometimes referred to as sounding nasal, or if you have heard voices that have a nasal, whiny sound, it means that resonance from the nose passages is occurring on sounds where it does not belong. Again a little experiment on your part can make this clear. Hold your nose and say "Ask Alberta to cross the path." Say it a couple of times this way and then a couple of times without holding your nose. The line should come out sounding fine either way, since there is no sound in any of the words requiring nasal resonance. Now again hold your nose and say "Ask Alberta to cross the cement path." Where did you get into trouble? Naturally, with the word "cement." Again with your nostrils pinched shut, try to say "Maybe we'll look at the moon, baby."

To repeat, then, any word that doesn't have an m, n, or ng will sound essentially the same, whether or not you've closed off the nasal passages. However, as you also found, if nasal resonance is needed and can't be supplied—the situation that occurs if you have a badly stuffed-up nose during a cold—we get the exact opposite of the whining over-nasal sound with a quality called "de-nasal" because it is devoid of any nasality whatever. The word "my" becomes indistinguishable from "by" and "maybe" turns out sounding the same as "baby."

Those are the two extremes that can happen with the nasal sounds. A much more common occurrence, and one of great importance to the actor, is that sometimes noticeable nasal resonance is given to a non-nasal sound because it is next to a nasal. Say the words "man, can, ran, hand, dance" and listen to determine whether the "a" sound in each word comes out without nasality. This can be accomplished only by taking the time to go to the required wide-open mouth position to make the "a" sound. This position raises the back part of the roof of your mouth (soft palate), shutting off the passage of air to the nasal cavities, thus preventing nasal resonance. To illustrate what can happen in using improper nasality try saying "man, can, ran, hand, dancing," opening your mouth as *little* as possible. Do you hear the difference?

Before we proceed to studying the articulators, it may be well to set down one absolutely rigid fact about speech that you will need to keep in mind as you progress in your study of speech for the stage as well as for ordinary conversational use. It is this: Whatever sound you *make* is the sound you'll *get*. That may sound like a threat, but it's also a promise.

This fact makes it possible for people to improve their speech, learn dialects, do vocal imitations, and learn to pronounce foreign languages correctly. If you haven't yet read *Pygmalion* by Bernard Shaw, put it at the top of your reading list. Eliza says in her Cockney accent, "I want to be a lady in a flower shop 'stead of selling at the corner of Tottenham Court Road, but they won't take me unless I can talk more genteel." She was right. So she changed the sounds she was

making and got a whole new sound, but it took hours of drilling and hard, hard work.

Essentially there is only one correct way to form a particular sound, and it is different from the formation of any other sound. You can give yourself a southern accent on the words "down south" simply by changing the "ow" sound to a different formation. Instead of making the "ow" out of the two sounds "ah" and "oo," make the first sound the "a" as in "cat" and then add "oo." If you live in the South, try the reverse procedure and notice how it changes the sound of the word. To illustrate another southern-northern variation, substitute the single sound of "ah" each time the diphthong "I" (a combination of "ah" "ee"—try it and see) occurs in this line, "I went to a fine high school." If you use only the first of the two sounds in "I" you find yourself saying, "Ah went to a fahn hah school."

The other determining factors in the sound you will get are the work of the articulators. These are the lips, tongue, and teeth. The teeth are not active articulators, since they don't change position, but it is clearer to list them since they are part of describing the action of the other two. For instance, if you know people who have spoken only Spanish for some time before learning English, you know that they have difficulty learning to pronounce the "v" sound, since there is no comparable sound in Spanish. As a result the word "voice" comes out "boice"—the nearest Spanish equivalent being "b" for "v." "Victory" comes out "bictory." The lips come together to form a "b" sound, and it is impossible to make a "v" sound unless the upper teeth touch the lower lip. Try it. The "tough" character saying "dese, dem, and dose" is forming a "d" sound by keeping his tongue inside his mouth instead of letting it come *between* the upper and lower teeth as it must to form the sound "th."

Unlike the vowels, which all have vocal sound and are therefore designated as "voiced," some of the consonants are "un-

Another scene from the University of Redlands production of Romeo and Juliet, *directed by Albert and Bertha Johnson.*

voiced." Simply make the *sound* for the following letters, as opposed to naming the letter; for example, the letter "k" is called "kay" but its *sound* has no voicing. Make just the sound and you will come out with an unvoiced "kuh"; thus the *sound* for the letters f, p, t, k, ch, sh, h, s, and wh have no vocal sound, but are a variety of shapings of a puff of air. Try each of them.

Now try shaping the original unvoiced puff for a sound and put a growl underneath it. Start with "fff" then put a growl underneath and you'll be making "vvv." Follow through now with these pairs, first with the shaped puff of air and then the voiced form you must have to change the sound: "puh" (unvoiced) "buh" (voiced), "tuh" (unvoiced), "duh" (voiced), "kuh" —"guh," "sss"—"zzz." These are some illustrations of the subtle and yet very precise differences in production that bring forth a totally different sound.

Now back to a point that was stated several pages back; let me say again that proper enunciation of the English language is more dependent on opening your mouth *wide* than on any other single factor. The common errors of sloppy diction such as "jist" for "just," "ketch" for "catch," "becuz" for "because," and voice problems such as lack of tone, nasality, poor projection, too rapid rate can be largely overcome if you make yourself *open your mouth wide enough to form the vowel sounds accurately.* When you begin doing this you may feel you resemble the wide-jawed look of a hippopotamus. Check in a mirror and you'll find you don't.

Try this sentence, "Mr. Hammer said that with luck there is a chance you just might catch the afternoon rather than the night plane." Now read it aloud again, with your index finger on the top of your nose and your thumb underneath your chin. If you are opening your mouth wide enough to make the sounds correctly your thumb and forefinger will be very actively and widely stretching apart. It is possible to say this

sentence so that it can be understood, scarcely opening your mouth at all. But you are not practicing to be a ventriloquist— you are working to develop correct and effective speech as an actor. Adequate opening of the mouth is not only essential for correct enunciation, but also contributes to facial expression, good vocal quality, and proper volume.

The Work Assignments at the end of the chapter include detailed exercises for relaxation, breathing, and the developing of resonance and projection. Stay with the practice and work assignments, never skipping a day.

That all-important matter of projection —being easily heard by every member of the audience—is not a separate vocal attribute that can be developed by itself. As you realize, it is made up of all the elements we have talked about thus far—proper breathing, ample resonance, exact articulation. To these will be added appropriate vocal quality, inflection, and pitch variation. Sometimes, however, the actor finds himself still being told "I can't hear you" or "Louder!" This may be a matter of the placement or focus of your voice. If you have access to a large classroom or an auditorium, practice speaking with the back row serving as the target toward which you are directing the words. This does not mean yelling, but rather it means consciously directing the sounds you are speaking, and aiming them at the farthest point in the room. Try visualizing a line of little cardboard ducks, like those in a shooting gallery, running along the back of the hall you're speaking in and make every *important* word you say (not every little if, and, or but) knock down one of the ducks. This will aid your ability to focus.

Speaking is an energetic activity, and basically the volume or loudness is dependent on the energy with which the sounds are produced. But this energizing is not applied at a constant level. If you've ever watched a kitten making successive leaps at a piece of string as it is drawn across the floor, you have a good illustration of the speaking process in its projected form. The breathing is energized, even when it is merely waiting to be used. The attack on words is a series of pounces of varying lengths and intensities, and the tension needed to supply the pounce comes from the diaphragm.

WORK ASSIGNMENT

Diaphragm Breathing

1. Stand erect, feet slightly apart. Tense muscles of toes, ankles, calves, knees, thighs, hips, waist, chest, shoulders, arms, wrists, fingers. Tense each set of muscles individually and hold the tension in each set as you progress. Extend arms above head as you tense arms, wrists, fingers. Hold with tension in all muscles for a mental count of three, then relax suddenly and completely, bending at the waist, arms hanging limp, head down. Repeat.

2. Standing with weight on both feet, and with shoulders relaxed, place the palms of your hands against the lower rib cage so finger tips are nearly touching. Open your mouth, and by pressing hard with your hands force all the air out of your lungs. You should be able to hear the air being expelled—a sort of prolonged "huuh"—unvoiced, but audible. When you have all the air squeezed out, suddenly release the pushing pressure but keep your hands on your ribs and feel them expand as air rushes into your chest cavity. Do it again. Now try it without forcibly expelling the air. Simply place the hands as before and take in a relaxed normal breath (not a deep breath). If your fingers move apart a little as the rib cage expands you are beginning to use correct breathing, but if the fingers stay put and the shoulders and upper chest rise you are using upper chest or "cla-

vicular" breathing instead of diaphragm. This may persist even after you begin to get rib-cage expansion, but it will decrease and disappear as the rib-cage expansion increases.

3. When you are able to get a little expansion at the base of the rib cage, without the shoulders rising, go on to this routine: With hands on rib cage, breathe in on a mental count of 4 (do not count aloud), hold 4, and exhale on 4. Increase the count to 6 after a few days, and then to 8.

4. Place hands on rib cage, finger tips nearly touching. Feel rib expansion as you take a catch breath, with your mouth open, and rib contraction as you slowly count aloud to 5. Be sure you exhale *all* breath on the count. Take a catch breath and count aloud to 10, then increase the count to 15. Repeat the series three times.

5. As soon as you are able to see and feel the expansion without placing your hands on your rib cage, begin to do exercise #3 as you walk. Not just walking around the house, but walking to school or on campus or to church or to the store. This will cut down on your conversation with friends, but just explain that you can't talk because you are practicing breathing. That should hold them. This is the most important step toward making diaphragm breathing involuntary, and for several weeks you must practice it consciously and conscientiously. Use the 4 count until it is easy, then proceed to 6 and 8, *eliminating* the holding count. Begin to alternate a half block of walking using an extended count (6 or 8) with a half block using your normal respiration rate, and gradually resume your normal respiration rate completely as the diaphragm breathing becomes automatic. Now you may also resume conversation in transit.

6. As you continue using exercise #3 without placing hands on the rib cage, con-

clude each brief exercise period by reading a section of *The Twelve Days of Christmas*. Use each section for at least three days of practice, even if you are able to read the final one on one breath right away. If you're a beginner at diaphragm breathing this is unlikely, to say the least. It is easy to cheat, however, without meaning to, because all of us just naturally take another breath when we need more air. Check to be sure you are not taking little catch breaths along the way. The purpose of the exercise is also to increase the volume and resonance of your voice, so be sure to use up *all* the breath you have as you say each successive "day." Don't go on to the next "day" until you can do the one you are on easily on one breath, and with a good full voice.

Important: Practice periods should be short (only one or two minutes at first), but *many* times per day. You will have to pace yourself on these assignments. It will probably take two or three weeks to get to #3 if you have never used diaphragm breathing. Exercises #3 and #4 should be continued up to and throughout the rehearsal period, even after you have arrived at #5, which is, of course, the major step.

The first day of Christmas my true love sent to me a partridge in a pear tree.

The second day of Christmas my true love sent to me two turtle doves and a partridge in a pear tree.

The third day of Christmas my true love sent to me three French hens, two turtle doves, and a partridge in a pear tree.

The fourth day of Christmas my true love sent to me four calling-birds, three French hens, two turtle doves, and a partridge in a pear tree.

The fifth day of Christmas my true love sent to me five gold rings. Four calling-birds, three French hens, two turtle doves, and a partridge in a pear tree.

The sixth day of Christmas my true love sent to me six geese a-laying, five gold rings. Four calling-birds, three French hens, two turtle doves, and a partridge in a pear tree.

The seventh day of Christmas my true love sent to me seven swans a-swimming, six geese a-laying, five gold rings. Four calling-birds, three French hens, two turtle doves, and a partridge in a pear tree.

The eighth day of Christmas my true love sent to me eight maids a-milking, seven swans a-swimming, six geese a-laying, five gold rings. Four calling-birds, three French hens, two turtle doves, and a partridge in a pear tree.

The ninth day of Christmas my true love sent to me nine drummers drumming, eight maids a-milking, seven swans a-swimming, six geese a-laying, five gold rings. Four calling-birds, three French hens, two turtle doves, and a partridge in a pear tree.

The tenth day of Christmas my true love sent to me ten pipers piping, nine drummers drumming, eight maids a-milking, seven swans a-swimming, six geese a-laying, five gold rings. Four calling-birds, three French hens, two turtle doves, and a partridge in a pear tree.

The eleventh day of Christmas my true love sent to me eleven ladies dancing, ten pipers piping, nine drummers drumming, eight maids a-milking, seven swans a-swimming, six geese a-laying, five gold rings. Four calling-birds, three French hens, two turtle doves, and a partridge in a pear tree.

The twelfth day of Christmas my true love sent to me twelve lords a-leaping, eleven ladies dancing, ten pipers piping, nine drummers drumming, eight maids a-milking, seven swans a-swimming, six geese a-laying, five gold rings. Four calling-birds, three French hens, two turtle doves, and a partridge in a pear tree.

Work Assignments

Relaxation

1. Stand erect, feet slightly apart. Tense muscles of toes, ankles, calves, knees, thighs, hips, waist, chest, shoulders,

arms, wrists, fingers. Tense each set of muscles individually and hold the tension in each set as you progress. Extend arms above head as you tense arms, wrists, fingers. Hold with tension in all muscles for a mental count of three, then relax suddenly and completely, bending at waist, arms hanging limp, head down. Repeat.

2. With body erect, raise arms over head, palms facing. Rise on toes and sway arms from left to right in a half circle. Do not bend knees, or body at hips. Keep arms and hands relaxed throughout, using just enough muscle power to move arms. Movement should be done slowly.

3. Spread feet apart to a comfortable degree, hold arms out in front of you, palms down, and sway shoulders from left to right and return. Use as big a circle as the fixed stance permits. All muscles relaxed. Feet flat on floor.

4. Clasping hands back of neck, with feet apart, swing elbows from left to right, and return. Repeat. Again keep feet flat on floor.

5. Keeping arms in front of body, permit fingers of left hand to clutch fingers of right hand, hook fashion. With forearm perpendicular to upper arm, pull vigorously until tension is maximum; hold. Completely relax after each exercise.

6. Roll head slowly, in circular movement. Reverse movement. All muscles relaxed as possible.

7. Relax the neck and throat muscles by dropping the head forward and rolling it from side to side, in a circular motion with mouth open and jaw relaxed. Then practice the following sentences, keeping the throat as relaxed as possible.
    a. Roll out the barrel.
    b. Slowly go the boats.
    c. How now brown cow.
    d. Hold the golden bowl.
    e. The cool blue moon.

8. On the following words, smile on the words with the vowel "e" and drop the lower jaw on the other vowel sounds. See saw, Kee kaw, Mee maw, Ye yawl, We wowl, Fee faw, Lee law, Mee mo, Ne noo, Kee kow.

9. In the following sentences articulate as distinctly as possible, using plenty of breath support on each sentence. Keep throat and jaw relaxed.
    a. Are you copper bottoming them, my man?
    b. No, I am aluminum bottoming them, mum.
    c. The British pronunciation is pretty brittle but it is brilliant and very clear.
    d. Shape the words with your lips and let the language flow prettily, but don't let yourself sound pedantic.
    e. The trick is to touch each word lightly yet with precision and clarity.

Chapter III

USING THE VOICE

The second Great American Fault so far as speech is concerned is the use of monotone or limited pitch range. The first Great Fault, described in the preceding chapter, is failure to open the mouth wide enough, and it is a major contributor to this second one —monotonous vocal pitch.

Pitch simply means how high or how low the tone is—where the sound lies in terms of the frequency-vibration scale.

An interesting point of contrast between the use of the singing voice and the use of the speaking voice is that in singing one moves from pitch to pitch mainly by steps or jumps. The speaking voice makes great use of glides to accomplish pitch variation. Gliding or slurring from one note to another is actually painful to hear in singing if it is incorrectly done, but the use of glide is one of the techniques you must cultivate to have a flexible, expressive speaking voice. The opposite of monotone is variety, and you will need to stretch to much greater limits the range of pitches you are now using.

Once again there are no magic tricks to do this, and also no especially difficult techniques. In fact, the answer to the question, "How do I get vocal variety?" is: "You *put* it there."

Look at this line from Robert Frost's "Stopping by Woods on a Snowy Evening":

Whose woods these are I think I know,

Read it aloud, listening to the pitch changes in your voice. Did you use any, other than the pitch drop to indicate the end of the statement?

We all have a certain pitch level that we use more than any other; it is simply the one that is most comfortable and so becomes habitual. This habitual pitch is always nearer to the bottom of the whole range of pitches on which we can speak than it is to the top, so the adding of pitch variety is going to require opening up and using your higher register. This applies to men as well as women, and does not mean that you will be working to raise the habitual pitch level. On the contrary, your habitual pitch is probably getting somewhat lower through relaxation and proper breathing. You will simply be beginning to *use* higher ranges that have been there all the time, waiting to be used.

Now let's go back to that line of Robert Frost's and impose a melody on it. I do not mean a singing melody but a speaking melody, made up of planned changes in pitch level. Start at the very top pitch that you can speak on without squeaking and then come right down the scale until you end up on your lowest pitch for the final word.

33

Whose woods these are I think I know,

Try it again and really reach way up for that top one, taking care not to come down the scale so rapidly that you hit your lowest possible pitch before the final word of the line. In terms of pitch changes, a "pitch pattern" or "melody pattern" for what you have just done would look like this:

```
Whose
    woods
        these
            are
                I
                    think
                        I
                            know
```

Try the line again with these pitch variations:

```
Whose woods
                think
            I       I
    these are
                        know
```

And this melody:

```
                think
        woods           I
                I
Whose       these are           know
```

Now let's try the whole first stanza of the poem, trying to follow closely the changes in pitch that are indicated for each line. You will need to read it slowly.

```
Whose
                think
        woods           I
                I       know
            these are

        house           vil
His       is in the         lage though
```

```
He
    will
        not
            see
                me stopping here


        watch
To      his woods fill up with snow.
```

This arbitrary imposing of pitch changes no doubt sounds extreme and artificial when you first try it, but with exercise and practice you will be able to employ a wide range of pitch changes in a way that will be a natural enhancement of the meaning of the words. You must train your ear to be aware of monotony in sound, both in yourself and in others. In early rehearsals of the play, listen consciously and carefully to be sure that when you enter a scene you do not fall into the same pitch that the other characters may have set. If a couple of actors start a scene off with a monotonous pitch pattern and everyone on entering picks it up, the performance is not likely to be referred to as "sparkling." This fault occurs frequently, especially in amateur groups. Pray you, avoid it.

As you know, we have many different forms of written punctuation to indicate a pause: comma, period, colon, semicolon, dash, a series of dots, are all forms that indicate some kind of stop. But suppose I gave you a sentence and asked you to read it with a comma in the middle of it, and then asked you to read it again with a semicolon in the middle. It would come out sounding just the same or so nearly so that I would not be able to say, "Ah, that time you used a semicolon!" In both cases, there would be a pause.

The use of pauses of varying lengths is one of the major means of punctuating vocally, and very often these pauses have little relation to the punctuation on the printed page. Written punctuation is given for *visual* clarity, and the process of absorbing the meaning visually from a printed page is quite different from the process of getting the meaning from something you *hear*. In the latter case it becomes the responsibility of the speaker to supply punctuation by expert, meaningful use of (1) pitch pattern, (2) pauses, (3) emphasis, and (4) vocal quality. The whole process of communication depends on the receiver's understanding what the sender's message is, so it is of utmost importance that you, the actor, be able to phrase your message so it is completely understandable to the receivers—your fellow actors and your audience.

To illustrate for yourself in simple terms the use of pitch pattern to give different meanings to the same line, try saying this sentence in such a way that it will give the *meaning* that follows it in parentheses:

Say this aloud	*to mean this*
I'd rather not go.	(Please, don't make me go!)
I'd rather not go.	(And I'm not going to go.)

Probably you stressed the words "rather" and "go" in both cases, and perhaps your vocal quality didn't change noticeably, but I'm sure your pitch pattern for the second meaning was quite different from the first.

Try the Robert Frost line—first to mean, "I'm not quite sure, but I believe I know who owns this land."

Whose woods these are I think I know

Now read it to say, "Boy, do I know who owns this land, and I'm out to get even with him!" This time you probably used variations in all four of the techniques for establishing meaning. In this particular poem, of course, the first meaning is the correct one, but there are any number of other meanings you might give, still using exactly the same words.

When you said the line, did you by any chance use a pause that is not indicated in the written punctuation? For both readings you may have used a slight hesitation after the first four words, "Whose woods these are." Try it again, consciously using the pause, and notice how it helps to make the meaning clear. In this case, then, we are *adding* oral punctuation that is not indicated in the written punctuation.

To see the opposite procedure in which we *omit* the use of written punctuation, read these lines by Robert Browning, observing the written pause after "oh," and continuing *without* pause after the first line:

> Oh, to be in England
> Now that April's there

Now try it again, leaving out the pause after "oh" and using it instead where there is none indicated—after the word "England." Better?

To summarize this very important point, then, the punctuation you find on the written page is not *necessarily* the punctuation you will use in reading or speaking the words aloud. You will use pauses where they most effectively bring out and amplify the meaning when the words are heard, not seen.

Generally in considering emphasis or stress, one thinks of words that are underlined or are printed in italics or in capital letters. This indicates that they are to be hit harder or read louder, or in some way given additional importance. This emphasizing of the important words in a thought is not limited to those that have some special punctuation. This is what we do all the time in all forms of speaking to make our meaning clear. Although we do use added volume as one means of emphasis, several other techniques are available that you, as an interpreter and actor, will be using much more because of their greater flexibility and subtlety. These we will call "lift" and "elongation." In other words, raising the pitch of the important word, and hanging onto the vowel sound so the word lasts longer. Try this sentence: "It's not orange, it's not purple, it's not yellow, it's *blue*." Did you find that in order to get the proper stress you lifted the pitch and also lengthened the word "blue?"

You will find that very often words to be lifted and elongated occur in clusters of two or three, rather than singly. Let's look at the poem "Light" by Frances Bourdillon for illustrations of this point. The italicized single words and clusters are the ones to be stressed.

> The *night* has a *thousand eyes*
> And the *day* but *one,*
> Yet the *light* of the *bright world dies*
> With the *dying sun.*

> The *mind* has a thousand eyes
> And the *heart* but one,
> Yet the *light* of a *whole life dies*
> When *love* is done.

As you read it aloud, try to identify which technique or combination of techniques you are using. Although lift and elongation are most frequently used together, you may find, for example, that on the word "love" in the final line, you have merely lifted the pitch to give the word the needed stress. Elongation in this case is not necessary to make the meaning clear and would destroy the rhythm of the poem.

The fourth consideration in using the voice to bring out the meaning is vocal quality. Since vocal quality is largely the result of emotional implication or mood in the material, it usually derives more from inner motivating forces than from applied techniques. Notice how the emotional tone of this first stanza of "Do Not Go Gentle into That Good Night" by Dylan Thomas determines the vocal quality:

> Do not go gentle into that good night,
> Old age should burn and rave at close of day;
> Rage, rage against the dying of the light.

Compare that vocal quality with the one you use as you read "Four Little Foxes" by Lew Sarett:

> Speak gently, Spring, and make no sudden sound;
> For in my windy valley, yesterday I found
> New-born foxes squirming on the ground—
>   Speak gently.

> Walk softly, March, forbear the bitter blow;
> Her feet within a trap, her blood upon the snow,
> The four little foxes saw their mother go—
>   Walk softly.

> Go lightly, Spring, oh, give them no alarm;
> When I covered them with boughs to shelter them from harm;
> The thin blue foxes suckled at my arm—
>   Go lightly.

> Step softly, March, with your rampant hurricane;
> Nuzzling one another, and whimpering with pain,
> The new little foxes are shivering in the rain—
>   Step softly.

Although we are not mainly concerned in this book with the reading of poetry, it is one of the best of all materials to use in developing a flexible, expressive voice. So while we are on the subject, here is a plan that might be titled "Almost-Instant Good Poetry Reading." Give it a try, even if (or especially if) you think you don't like poetry:

1. Select a fairly short poem and copy it in paragraph form. That is, do not indicate where the lines and stanzas end as it is printed. Copy it into one block and do not

put in any of the printed punctuation except periods.

2. Read it aloud from this copy, seeking only to find out exactly what the poem says.

3. Read it again, noticing and marking with a caret (ᴧ) the places where you are pausing to bring out meaning. Mark with a slash (/) a pause that indicates the end of a thought. This is not always a repetition of what you did in Step 1, since sometimes the writer has not indicated a thought ending where you may find the need for one. *Underline* the words you wish to lift and/or elongate.

4. Start at the beginning of the paragraph and tell, in your own words, what the poem says.

5. Read it again, with the exact words of the poet, observing the pauses and stresses as you have marked them.

6. Make final adjustments, if needed, and try it out on somebody.

That's the end of the course, but naturally applying it just once won't do the trick. After you have used this method a number of times, you will find that you automatically apply it as you look at a poem, without having to go to the trouble of copying it. To get you started here's an example, using the first part of "Home, Thoughts from Abroad" by Robert Browning:

Original

Oh, to be in England
Now that April's there,
And whoever wakes in England
Sees, some morning, unaware,
That the lowest boughs and the brush-
    wood sheaf
Round the elm-tree bole are in tiny leaf,
While the chaffinch sings on the orchard
    bough
In England — now

Your Copy

Oh to be in England now that April's there and whoever wakes in England sees some morning unaware that the lowest boughs and the brushwood sheaf round the elm-tree bole are in tiny leaf while the chaffinch sings on the orchard bough in England now!

To try to insure that you'll follow through on reading this, I'll tell you that the word "bole" means the trunk of the tree, so you don't have to go and look it up.

Marked Copy

Oh to be in England ᴧ now that April's there / and whoever wakes in England ᴧ sees ᴧ some morning ᴧ unaware ᴧ that the lowest boughs ᴧ and the brushwood sheaf round the elm-tree bole ᴧ are in tiny leaf / while the chaffinch sings on the orchard bough / in England / now!

Of course the pauses are not all the same in length. The one after "elm-tree bole" is very short, or you may wish to leave it out entirely. If you use this pause, perhaps you would omit the one after "boughs" or make it very short. The two marked as thought endings at the close of this section of the poem—after "orchard bough" and "in England"—are long ones.

I am reluctant to leave the subject of poetry. Although you can get great enjoyment from reading it silently, it is meant to be read aloud, and in hearing it read well lies the most complete appreciation of the work. It's a wonderful form of solitary entertainment, too, in which you are not only the star but also the audience. It is a concentrated literary form—its wordings spare and carefully chosen. Consider these twenty-three words by Rebecca McCann, entitled "Pride":

I threw my coat around me
To take a haughty leave,
But my hand went through the lining
Instead of down the sleeve!

Now in your own words, say aloud what the poem tells about you, the situation you were in, what happened, and how you felt. It's not likely you'll be able to do it without using 100 or 200 more words than Miss McCann used.

Finally, a word of caution in choosing a poem to read aloud. If you come to something you don't understand, and after trying your best to figure it out you cannot say *clearly* in your own words what it means, then consult reference books or some person who may be able to help you. If you are still unable to arrive at a plausible and workable meaning for the passage, don't use the material. Failure to observe this cardinal rule is what has produced so much awful poetry reading. It leads to adopting a sort of sad, syrupy voice—purported to convey the "beauty" of the words, but actually to obscure the fact that the reader hasn't the foggiest notion what he's talking about.

The rules for getting a line *right,* whether it's poetry or prose, Shakespeare, classical drama, modern, or whatever, are firmly grounded in your having the answer to this question: "What does it *mean*?"

WORK ASSIGNMENTS

1. Continue daily use of #1, #2 and #3 at the end of Chapter II.
2. Say the line, "Oh, what a beautiful morning" in a full voice at your habitual pitch. Now repeat the line, each time taking a lower starting pitch until you have reached the bottom of your register.
3. Again say the line at your habitual pitch. Repeat the line, each time taking a higher starting pitch until you have reached the very top of your range. Did you find that you had much more area in which to go up than you did to go down?
4. Take a short poem, a passage from a speech, or a portion of a children's story and make a pitch pattern graph, using short lines at various heights to indicate the pitch level for each word.

Where you have a glide from one pitch to another within a word, indicate it by a curved line.

5. Now mark the passage for pauses, using a caret for the pauses within lines and a slash for the pause indicating the end of a thought. This should be done with regard only for the pauses you are using when you read it aloud, rather than the punctuation that is printed. Read the passage over several times, aloud, observing your pause marks and making changes as you find better ways of phrasing to bring out the meaning.
6. Mark the passage for words you wish to lift and/or elongate by underlining them. Note that very often you will have stress phrases made up of two or three words rather than just single words.
7. Practice the selection aloud several times, concentrating on each area separately (pitch pattern, pauses, vocal quality, and stress); then put them all to work at the same time to achieve what you feel is an interesting, meaningful reading.
8. If possible, make a tape recording of the selection. Listen to it in terms of the four specific areas as well as the overall effect and criticize it.
9. Practice the following sentences for projection. Note the tension in the diaphragm as you "pounce" on the important words, and strive to avoid throat tension.
   a. Ho there! Halt! Give me the message.
   b. I'll be walking the river path—slowly.
   c. "Government of the people, by the people, for the people shall not perish from the earth."
   d. "There, but for the grace of God, go I."
   e. You said you would help them. Do it now!

10. Listen to recordings of scenes or speeches from plays. Many school libraries and almost all public libraries have such records. It will be most meaningful if you can have a copy of the scene to look at as you listen. Notice what the actors do specifically in terms of pitch change, pause, stress, and voice quality. Scenes from Shakespeare are excellent for this study. It would be interesting to compare two actors on the same material, noting the differences and evaluating which you think is better, and why. Try to make this a useful exercise in critical listening—identifying what you find is especially effective as well as areas you feel do not come off well.

    Note: For reading exercises, be sure to use material that was meant to be spoken or read aloud, not a novel, newspaper item, or something else intended mainly for silent reading. The vocabulary in material for silent reading is more complex, and the sentence structure longer and more complicated.

11. Use the following lines from *I Remember Mama* by John Van Druten as an exercise in varying meaning. It is written for a girl, but by deleting the words in parentheses it can be used just as well by a young man.

    For as long as I could remember, the house on Steiner Street had been home. Papa and Mama had both been born in Norway, but they came to San Francisco because Mama's sisters were here. All of us were born here. Nels, the oldest (and the only boy)—my sister Christine—and the littlest sister, Dagmar. It's funny, but when I look back, I always see Nels and Christine and myself looking almost as we do today. I guess that's because the people you see all the time stay the same age in your head. Dagmar's different. She was always the baby—so I see her as a baby. Even Mama—it's funny, but I always see Mama as around forty. She couldn't *always* have been forty. Besides us, there was our boarder, Mr. Hyde. Mr. Hyde was an Englishman who had once been an actor, and Mama was very impressed by his flowery talk and courtly manners. He used to read aloud to us in the evenings. But first and foremost, I remember Mama.

Decide on specific answers to these questions and try to make your reading give those answers:
  a. What do you feel about Mama?
  b. What is your attitude toward Dagmar?
  c. What did you think of Mr. Hyde?
  d. How were his "readings"?

Here are some suggestions to get you started. See if you can project one or two of these and find others.
  a. 1. She's the greatest!
     2. Mainly, that she just always seemed middle-aged.
  b. 1. I still have for her the special love one has for a darling, helpless baby.
     2. She was sort of a nuisance, as I guess all baby sisters can be.
  c. 1. I can't really remember, but I think of him now with kindly amusement.
     2. I wasn't at all impressed by him, even if Mama was. He not only lived there, we had to listen to him read!
  d. 1. They were a special treat that I looked forward to.
     2. They were pretty bad.

One could rather generally classify the "1" suggestions as positive, and the "2" suggestions as negative. If you try a number of readings using these suggestions, be sure to employ a mixture of the two in each reading, rather than using all negative or all positive.

And remember, we are not yet asking which interpretations would be right if you were acting the part, but working for flexibility and variety. Your voice must be *capable* of expressing what your mind and imagination *ask* it to express.

A duet in the production of The Fantasticks *by Tom Jones and Harvey Schmidt, given at South Eugene High School, Eugene, Ore., and directed by Edward Ragozzino.*

Chapter IV

BODY AND MOVEMENT

Think back over all the advice you've ever been given about posture, and begin to apply it now. I've never heard of posture instruction doing anyone any harm, no matter what the particular method or gimmick. Erect but relaxed and easy posture is the necessary framework for both good voice production and good movement.

The exercises you are doing daily for proper breathing should be helping a great deal in bringing you to good posture if you didn't already have it, since it isn't possible to get much rib expansion if you're standing with hunched shoulders and a caved-in chest. By the time you've been doing the breathing exercises for about two weeks (maybe less) you should have arrived at step 5. With this step you are now to be consciously using diaphragm breathing on a 6 or 8 count as you walk. Add to this your own favorite mental image, if that helps you to walk erect. Some of the old standbys are: (1) Imagine that a string is hitched to the top of your head and you are suspended from it in such a manner that your feet just comfortably touch the ground. (2) Imagine that you are carrying a large, not very heavy, well-balanced basket of produce on your head. (3) Consciously tuck your seat under you as if you were actually sitting as you walk. (4) Imagine that you have a fairly large book balanced on your head. With whatever image you adopt, be sure you don't

take on a rigid wooden-soldier posture. The aim is to walk tall, but easy.

Did you think when you became interested in acting that you would be practicing how to *breathe* and *talk* and *walk*? After all, you have been getting around, breathing and communicating for some years now. But I'm sure you are finding that these taken-for-granted abilities are like any other skill, and can be improved and enlarged beyond their primary functional purpose. The question is not whether you *can* talk, but how well you can learn to use your voice, and not whether you can cross from this door to that chair and sit down, but *how* you will do it.

If you were to make a straight line in the sand on a beach and then walk from the beginning of the line to the end your footprints would probably lie along each side of the line somewhat in this manner:

Ideally there is a slight toeing out, but as you see, the basic position is one that would have the feet close to each other but not quite touching as you stand to begin the walk. If it were possible to trace the movement of your head as you do this walk, it would indicate some movement up and down, but not much—not enough to spill the basket of produce, if that's what you're carrying on your head. Now from this standard walk, let's see what happens if we vary the basic foot position.

Go back to that line in the sand, or draw a chalk line on the floor if you don't have a beach handy—it will do just as well. Start your walk from the standard foot position and gradually widen the base as you proceed, like this:

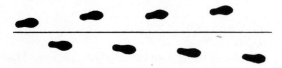

Try it once again and see if this progression toward a waddle makes you *feel* any different. Do you feel heavier? Does it give you a feeling of age, so that you find you are also inclined to let your shoulders droop?

Try walking along the line with your toes turned way out, and see what that does to the way you move and the way you feel. Try the walk with toes turned in. Walk the line using uneven pressure—heavy with the right and light with the left—and you will, of course, have a limp. Did you find that each different walk made you begin to *feel* different? Well, this ability of your body position and movement to lead you into a feeling is something you'll be using in depth and in infinite variety as you move into the building of a character.

Suppose that instead of keeping the basic foot position on each side of the line you were to place one foot directly ahead of the other, toes slightly turned out, so the pattern looked like this:

The accompanying graph of head movement with this walk would show no up and down movement whatsoever, but a perfectly straight, even line. You could carry a glass of water, either real or imaginary, on your

head and not spill it. This particular walk is sometimes referred to as the Grecian Tread, and as you try it notice that you must start the step with the pressure on the ball of your foot rather than the heel. When you see someone appear to roll across the stage in a hoop skirt, or float across in an elegant ball gown, this is what's going on underneath. With extremely exaggerated turning out of the toes this becomes the walk used by both men and women for certain styles of period plays, notably Restoration. This latter foot position—placing one directly in front of the other with toes turned out—is also the only way to come down a flight of stairs in a long gown and make it safely to the bottom.

For most purposes you will be using the easy, footprint-each-side-of-the-line walk, and you should be using it for all purposes of getting from place to place by foot, not just on stage. We will consider some suggestions on movement a little later on in the chapter, though of course the specific manner in which you move is rooted in the character you are playing.

At one time acting books contained chapters on the use of gestures and facial expression quite as if these were capable of being developed as an entity in themselves, independent of the character. The actor trained in this manner was very apt to use an overabundance of sweeping arm movements and considerable grimacing as proof to the audience that he was experiencing an emotion.

Gestures and facial expressions in realistic plays cannot be planned and imposed, line by line, but must spring naturally from an inner motivation. The chances are much greater that your director may suggest that you use fewer gestures than that he will ask you to add them. One of the hardest lessons to learn is that you look just fine standing still, arms at your sides, doing nothing, so long as you are listening with every cell and sinew and nerve-ending. When you are reacting with the truth and spontaneity that results from taking in what is going on, then the "right" gestures and facial expressions happen without conscious attention to them.

Now let us define the stage areas in which you, the actor, will be moving—first in terms of proscenium theatre. The proscenium stage is sometimes referred to as the picture-frame stage, since the audience is seated out front looking at action confined in the three walls of a set. The fourth wall is not there, since that is the framed opening that allows the play to be seen.

Now look at the script you selected as the basis for your acting study. You will find that the set is described in considerable detail at the opening of the play, and movements are suggested ranging all the way from a direction to glance a certain way to much larger movements of entering, leaving, and moving about on the stage. For instance, in the *Lawyer Lincoln* script you find such directions as "crossing UR to kitchen door," "her back is toward outside door ULC," "a face peers in at the window UC," etc. These must be considered in relation to the diagram of the set, which is called either a floor plan or ground plan. Nearly all printed plays have the ground plan in the back of the book, and if you are using *Lawyer Lincoln,* you will find it printed on page 80 of *Directing.*

The ground plan is drawn from a viewpoint directly above the stage—a bird's-eye view of the set in terms of the placement of doors, windows, other architectural features such as stairway, fireplace, and the exact location of all the furniture.

At the moment, however, our concern is not with the filled-in ground plan, but with a consideration of the areas into which the empty stage is divided. Here is a ground plan divided into the six major designations of area with the names of each written in full and also in abbreviated form, as most commonly used in play books:

UR UP RIGHT	UC UP CENTER	UL UP LEFT
DR DOWN RIGHT	DC DOWN CENTER	DL DOWN LEFT

AUDIENCE

The first thing to note is that the directions Right (R) and Left (L) refer to the actor's right hand and left hand as he stands facing the audience. This never changes.

The second thing to note is that the areas at the back of the stage, farthest from the audience, are referred to as Up (U), whereas the areas at the front of the stage and nearest to the audience are referred to as Down (D).

Often combinations of the areas are used in a direction in order to pinpoint more accurately where you are to move. If you enter from a door Down Right (DR) and cross (X) to Up Left Center (ULC), you would arrive in an area upstage and midway between Center and Left.

If you are not now familiar with these basic stage divisions, study the diagram carefully and practice moving from one area to another in a room. Pick one wall to represent the audience and name aloud each area as you move into it. It is vitally important that you master the ability to interpret movement in terms of area as quickly as possible.

To add the next element we will introduce furniture into the ground plan, and also an entrance in the back wall UR. In the next diagram, then, there is a table C, door UR, and a chair DL. If your direction, either from the script or given you by the director says: "Enter UR X *above* table to chair DL," this is your pattern of movement:

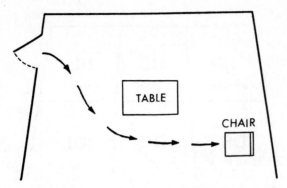

If, instead, the direction reads "Enter UR X *below* table to chair DL," this is your pattern:

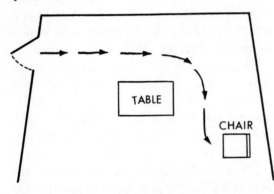

To put it into words, whenever "above" is used in a direction, it means you are to move *upstage* of the person or piece of furniture in your direct path. To cross "below" is to move *downstage* of them.

Next to be considered are the basic body positions in terms of relation to audience. When you are directly facing the audience your position is called "open"; when you have your back to them, it is called "closed." Between these two extremes of full front and full back are three intermediate designations on each side. These are ¼ R, profile R, ¾ R, and of course the same when you turn in the other direction: ¼ L, profile L, and ¾ L.

To tie together our three fundamental rules that (1) Right and Left always refer to the actor's R and L; (2) Upstage and Above are away from the audience; Downstage and Below are toward the audience; and (3) there are eight basic body positions in terms of degree of being "open" (facing toward the audience) or "closed" (facing away from the audience), examine these directions and the accompanying diagram:

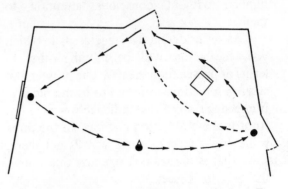

The actor is to enter UC, X to window R. After looking out the window X to DC, stand in completely closed body position. Then X 3 steps toward door DL. Stop, decide not to leave, take a closed turn, X above chair ULC, and exit UC. A second set of arrows indicates taking an open turn and Xing below chair ULC to exit UC. When you are sure you understand the moves, ask someone to read them off to you, slowly, as you walk through them.

If most of the information on stage areas and movement is new to you, this might be a good place to pause and spend sufficient time on the material just covered so that you feel sure you understand it and can accomplish the moves easily as the directions are read to you, or as you read them yourself from the book.

In a fairly open area, either at home or in a rehearsal room, arrange two chairs—preferably one straight back (#1) and one armchair (#2)—at a distance of about 6 to 8 feet from each other. Place one chair above the other in about this relationship:

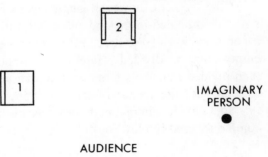

Here are your directions: Sit in chair #1, rise, X to chair #2, turn and address several lines of dialogue to an imaginary person DL. Then sit in chair #2. Rise and X to the person DL.

For the first rise from chair #1, did you jackknife in the middle, grasp the edges of the seat, and shove out of the chair? After crossing to the armchair and addressing the lines to the person DL, did you have to turn around to be sure just where the chair was before you sat? For the rise from the armchair did you grab both arms of the chair and hoist yourself out? If the answer to all three questions is "yes" that's not surprising, but there is a better way. Try this, step by step, and practice it a few times every day until you can do it easily and without awareness of each individual step.

1. Sit in chair #1. Put left foot slightly back of position of right foot and rise by using your leg muscles to push you up. Don't use your hands and arms to push. When you are upright, your weight should now be on the *right* foot.
2. Take the first step of your cross toward the armchair with your left (upstage) foot.
3. Cross to a position close enough to the armchair so that as you turn to speak to the person DL the back of your left leg is touching the chair. Sit without looking back of you—the chair will be there.
4. Rise, using the same technique as before, but reverse the foot positions and this time start with your right foot slightly back of the left. When you're upright, your weight should be on the left foot and you are ready to XR.

As you repeat the exercise, make note of these generalizations: You usually get off to a better start on a cross by taking the first step with the upstage foot, especially if the cross goes somewhat upstage. You can find this out for yourself by doing steps #1 and #2 of the exercise with reverse positions. Rise with the weight on the left foot and take

the first step toward the chair with right (downstage) foot. You may find yourself in a somewhat awkward twist. In kneeling, a position with the downstage knee on the floor is usually easier to get in and out of gracefully. In crossing to any piece of furniture on which you are going to sit, feel the edge of the piece touching the back of one or both of your legs before you sit.

Finally, here is a technique for a stage fall that, properly done, will not leave you battered and bruised.

1. If the fall is the result of a blow or a shot, "take" (react physically) with the area of the body that is supposed to be hit. If it's a faint, then of course you omit this step.
2. Let your legs go limp.
3. Drop sideways to the floor onto the *side* of the lower legs and knees.
4. Immediately roll back so that the hip also touches the floor.
5. As the hip touches the floor, fling the upper part of your body forward, chest down, with arms extended.
6. Don't let your feet fly up as your upper body goes down unless you're *supposed* to get a laugh.

You can learn a great deal about movement by becoming aware and observant of the way people move as they walk along a street on a warm sunny day, on a windy day, when they are in a hurry, when they are in love. Look around. And if you have ever heard it said that an actor should never turn his back to the audience, pay no attention. Nothing is more old-fashioned than actors addressing lines straight out toward the audience and making elaborate unnatural crosses to stay opened up. Take the crosses and turns that you would if the stage were actually a room. However, in the playing of your dialogue it is well to stay in as open a body position as is natural and possible, unless the director specifies a particular position he wishes you to take either to bring out a certain value or for an effect he wishes to accomplish in the overall composition of the stage picture. No doubt you have heard of actors "upstaging" one another—a very old and sneaky trick, accomplished when one actor, by small moves during a scene, gradually gets farther and farther upstage until the other actor, in order to address him, must turn his back to the audience. This can happen unintentionally also, so there is a double awareness needed not to be guilty of upstaging and to be on guard so that it doesn't happen to you.

One final and very important rule about movement is this: Generally speaking, you move only on your own lines—not when someone else is speaking. There are some exceptions, but unless a move is specifically indicated by your director, your business is listening while someone else is speaking.

Considerations of the differences in area designation and movement for the arena stage and the thrust stage will be examined in later chapters. Right now you need to learn your DL's and UR's and DRC's.

WORK ASSIGNMENTS

1. Repeat the walking procedure described on page 43, trying to determine whether your present walk needs some correction.
2. Add a mental image for good posture to your count breathing as you walk from place to place during the day.
3. Sketch a basic ground plan of a stage, and divide it into the six major areas. Mark each with the full designation and also the correct er abbreviation.
4. In a cleared area, without furniture, execute the moves below. If possible, work with a partner on the next two as-signments so you can check each other's accuracy.

X from DR through C to UL
X from DR above C to UL
X from UC to RC to DL to UR
X from UC to DC

5. Place a chair DR, facing L, a chair ULC facing ¼ R, and a piece of furniture to indicate a table C and execute the following moves:
Sit in chair ULC, rise, X above table to chair DR, and sit.
Sit in chair ULC, rise, X around L side of chair to above chair, face profile R.
Sit in chair DR, rise, X around R side of chair to UR, take a position facing ¾ L, then open up.
X from chair DR, above table to above chair ULC, come around L side of chair, and sit.
XL from chair DR, below table, and sit in chair ULC.
Move about at random, naming each area and body position as you use it.
6. Consult the play you are using to see if it has a ground plan. If it does not, sketch one for yourself from the set description.
7. Read the entire play slowly, with the ground plan before you, *carefully noting all stage directions.* Try to visualize these moves as you read them.
8. Spend a lot of time on the exercises within the chapter and in the Work As-signments. This is rather complicated material when you first meet it, but you should go into rehearsal with the ability to interpret and accomplish movement directions accurately and swiftly.

Chapter V

SENSE MEMORY AND EMOTION RECALL

Acting a part should be literally a "total" experience, for you will need to bring to it every resource you can possibly command and a concentration of thought and energy surpassing anything you have used before.

Designate a day for yourself as "Sense Awareness Day" and carry around a little notebook to record some of the actual physical stimuli to which you respond. The list will be a long and varied one, containing such things as alarm-clock ring, shaggy rug felt soft to bare feet, smelled bacon, cool air made me shiver when I got out of shower, felt glow-y after brisk rub with towel, sand in sneakers, orange juice was sour, etc., etc. To each of these stimuli you will be reacting specifically, as each situation is interpreted through your senses of sight, hearing, taste, touch, and smell.

Sometimes, on stage, the actor is called upon to react to an actual, direct sense stimulus: Someone yells at you loud enough so you really jump, a "heavy" object you pick up actually weighs 20 pounds, the mink coat borrowed for the big entrance *is* soft and gorgeous. But the art of acting is in truth the art of make believe, and that word "believe" is the loaded end of the phrase. Unless you can believe in the truth and reality of what you are doing, certainly no audience will. To do this requires an acute sharpening of every kind of awareness; right

now our focus is on the physical reactions to stimuli, which brings us to another tremendously important sense called "kinesthesia."

Kinesthesia is also known as "muscle sense," described in the dictionary as "a sensation of position, movement, tension, etc., of parts of the body." At its most elementary level it is this muscle sense that does a lot of the work of memorization for you. During the early rehearsals you will find that walking through the moves as you practice at home helps you remember the lines. Of course this is a matter of associating the line with the movement intellectually as well. The kinesthetic sense was at work when you did the exercises in Chapter III and found that changing the muscular set in walking began to induce a different feeling.

Don't take the suggestion about giving yourself a Sense Awareness Day to mean that it is a kind of stunt to be tried out once and then dropped. The intent is that a day of acutely focusing your attention on sense perception should serve to open up a continuing awareness of these sensations and reactions so that they become a vast storehouse of sense memory.

These you will use sometimes as direct applications. Suppose you are playing a scene in which cascades of confetti snow are being blown at you as you struggle to find

49

shelter and safety. If you have a sense memory of being out in a howling blizzard, you will use it to recall the sting of the snow on your face, the numbness of your hands and feet, the fatigue in every muscle as you fought against the wind. If you are playing Elizabeth Barrett in *The Barretts of Wimpole Street* and must drink a tankard of porter, which is bitter and totally repugnant to you, you most surely will not drink something actually so bitter that it makes you choke and gag. But you might use a sense memory of having been forced to down a teaspoon of medicine that made you shudder and gasp for breath because it was so bitter.

The center of the effectiveness of this tool again goes back to finding the reality; not in going through a set of motions to imitate the response you felt, but in trying to actually re-create the response. This ability is like all the other skills you are setting out to develop. It will expand and sharpen with use as you consciously apply it, and finally it will become one of the steps in your preparation that you may not even realize you are using.

The storehouse of sense memory moves into another tremendous realm of usefulness as applied to behavior needed in response to situations whose characteristics have no direct relationship to the sense memory situation. In other words, ones in which the stimulus is different, but might elicit the same response. To return to the snowstorm memory, suppose you were playing a young man following lead after lead to clear the name of his father who was executed for a crime he did not commit—the situation of Mio in Maxwell Anderson's *Winterset*. As you are met with secretiveness, evasions, hostility in your fervent questioning of those who know who the guilty one is, the sense memory of pressing against a terrible force of wind and snow that makes your eyes sting and your body ache with physical frustration could be useful. Or the Captain, uttering the words that order the hanging of Billy Budd might use the sense memory of

having drunk a poisonous-tasting liquid, or taken a swallow of coffee so hot that it burned his tongue and throat.

These are but a few examples of how sense memory can work for you. The major applications for you to file in your thoughts now are: You must (1) become acutely aware of your responses to sense stimuli and (2) consciously and conscientiously apply them to either direct or related situations. The Work Assignments at the end of the chapter should be practiced with the actual stimulus whenever possible, and then rehearsed as a sense memory. Don't be limited by the suggestions given; many, many others will occur to you to add to the list.

All acting owes a great debt to Stanislavsky, who has been interpreted and misinterpreted by countless writers and directors and actors. He has given us the labels as well as the design for using many of the resources within ourselves, such as sense memory and emotion recall. Sense memory is of inestimable value to the individual not only as an actor but as a human being because of the demands made to *acquire* it. It forces us to attention and awareness. You cannot have a memory of something unless you have first experienced it. A rich ore filled with these nuggets of sensing surrounds us all the time, and we may extract them by intellectual decision—training ourselves to pay attention to them.

The gathering of resources to be used as emotion recall cannot be similarly done. Perception is part intellect, whereas emotion, at its *height,* leaves no room for intellect. At various stages we may be able to temper our feeling with reason, but not when we are totally in its grip. There is a reason for such descriptions as "madly" in love, "insanely" jealous, "deliriously" happy, "wild" with anger. They represent the absence of rationality. It follows, then, that we cannot stand aside and analyze for future use the anguish we feel when the puppy is sick or the parakeet dies. Recall of the emotion can only be reconstructed by minute, painstaking effort to revive in imagination each lesser feeling leading up to our grief, and making use of the sense memory, muscle sense, and any other tool that may induce the emotion.

Such recall of emotion is usually applied to a related situation rather than an identical one. An ability to recall the joy you felt when you saw the bicycle you had yearned for standing beside the Christmas tree might be used in a range of joy behavior encompassing an unexpected act of forgiveness, a quietly spoken word of praise, or a confession of love from someone *you* love. So it might be with the recall of the jealousy you felt at a party, the fright you experienced when you were "lost" while shopping with your mother in a crowded store, the anger over an unjust punishment, or the breathless feeling of awe you experienced on looking at something of exquisite beauty. Can you think, right now, of two situations that produced in you a powerful emotional reaction? Can you think of two that have been associated with gentler emotions, such as pleasant anticipation or a feeling of accomplishment?

Re-creating an emotion is one of the sources on which you may be able to draw in acting, but it is necessary that you grow beyond this. The only way an actor can create the truth of a character and keep it alive performance after performance is by being capable of kindling the emotion for each situation from within the character and action being played. And if the spark of inspiration does not always occur, he must have the techniques of his craft so in control that they will appear to produce the needed incandescence. When the concentration of the actor goes to the *recall* of something (which is inactive in terms of behavior) rather than the *playing* of something, the life and vigor and reality go out of the acting.

We are dealing now, as you realize, with elements of training and preparation to be used before you utter a single word in performance. Words are only one of the instruments for communicating what's going on, and they are not always the most powerful one; otherwise a person could read a play and get nearly as much impact from it as in seeing it acted. Your approach begins by listening with all your senses, and finding out what you are thinking, what you are feeling, what you are *doing,* underneath and through the words you are saying.

So the combining process begins here, with the tools of body and movement used in conjunction with the resources of mind and imagination, to produce feeling and emotion.

Think back to the exercises in previous chapters that have begun to apply this concept. You found that broadening the base of your walk gave you a different feeling than you got from a straightforward, vigorous walk. You found that reacting muscularly to a situation of cold reminds you of what it is to *feel* cold. Try this exercise, concentrating your attention on how you feel, rather than on the physical move:

Stand erect, trying to be as tall as you possibly can. Imagine that you are a king. Gradually let your body slump and finally sink to the floor. After a moment, strive to push up, lifting your body until you are again upright. Stretch tall, fling your arms upward, and spring from the floor.

Now try this one:

Cringe and glance over your shoulder to look behind you as you walk, imagining that you are being pursued. Gradually begin to stand erect. Finally walk around the room with an exaggerated swagger, chest way out, chin way up. Imagine that you are the *champ.*

You realize how foolish and futile it would be if someone were to put you on a stage and say "be frightened" or "act sad" or "feel happy." Even if you stood there and recalled a vivid situation that had given you that emotion before, you still must find the means for translating it into behavior—so where do you start? You start with a physical attitude, assuming posture, body positions, and movement that are visible evidences of the inner feeling.

A very old and variously interpreted theory of emotion is one called the James-Lange theory. Reduced to simple working terms for use in acting, it might be stated thus: You are afraid because you run, or, you are sad because you cry. In other words, the physical manifestation of the emotion comes first, and is *followed* by the feeling. Here are a couple of illustrations.

If you are driving a car and you see another car approaching at a rapid speed and far enough over the center line so that you must swerve to avoid a crash, your hands swing the wheel to the right, your foot goes to the brake, and you stop the car. *Then* the feeling of panic overwhelms you, and you are weak with fear.

When the football game is tied, 30 seconds to play, and the home team has fourth down and goal to go, you sit with clenched fists, hunched shoulders, furrowed brow, and all the physical attitudes of the tension you are feeling. The ball is snapped, there's a pile-up at the goal line, and as the referee's arms signal "Touchdown!" you leap to your feet, clap your hands, hug the person next to you, and a feeling of exhilaration sweeps through you. You don't sit there, feeling a great wave of exhilaration, and *then* leap to your feet, etc., etc.

The application of this concept to your creating of feeling and emotion is simply this —when the scene demands a certain emotion, in addition to your applying mind and imagination you will assume the postures, body positions, and movements that will lead you into the emotion.

Do a little observing in a classroom or in a group attending the theatre or a lecture. Note the various emotional attitudes you can spot before the program has even begun. The slumped posture, the bored facial expression, the limp hand holding the program tells you right off that the person will probably be bored and disinterested because he has pre-set that reaction by his physical attitude. And naturally the reverse is true, too. If you pre-set your mechanism to an alert, receptive attitude by assuming the postures of interest and animation, the chances are you'll feel that way.

There was a superb illustration of this theory in a cartoon which I saw several years ago. It was a series of six or eight sketches, without captions, showing a housewife, all smiles and humming happily as she stood at the kitchen sink starting to slice a huge bowlful of onions. Gradually the smile fades and the humming stops as the onions begin to irritate her eyes. Then actual tears begin to fall; she crosses with the bowl and knife to the kitchen table and sits down, sobbing uncontrollably. In the final sketch she has plunged the knife into her heart and lies toes up on the kitchen floor.

I'm not suggesting that you carry it *that* far, but take plenty of time on the Work Assignments for sense memory and emotion recall. Sometimes beginning actors are reluctant to work hard enough to really explore their possibilities. Your first few attempts may seem very unproductive, but if you are fully aware of what it is you are trying to do, you will gain greater facility and reality with each one you perform.

WORK ASSIGNMENTS

1. How are you progressing with your diaphragm breathing?
2. Collect the articles mentioned in the following exercises or similar ones that will be useful for sense memory practice. Be acutely perceptive of the sensations. Many will involve a combination of senses.

Taste a lemon.
Hold a piece of ice in your hand.

Smell ammonia.

Stroke a piece of fur.

Study the color of an orange.

Peel the orange.

Set an alarm clock to ring in a few minutes. Put it near you but not where you can see it, and go on to other exercises.

Put some perfume or shaving lotion on your hand and smell it.

Look at something silver, then something gold.

Put a small piece of butter in your mouth.

Pick up the electric iron. Feel the metal bottom when it is cold. Plug it in and continue testing the heat until it is too hot to touch.

Smell a carnation, or a crushed geranium leaf.

Listen to a clock tick.

Sit in a dark room, late at night, and listen to the sounds within the room and from outside.

On a very clear day study the blue of the sky.

Walk barefoot on a pebbly beach or on a gravel driveway.

Look at clouds.

3. Working from the list of things you have done, *imagine* the stimulus and try to re-create the sensation.

4. Try to re-create the following from memory:

   See sharp lightning.
   Wait for and hear the thunder.

Smell pine trees.

Feel a soft wooly blanket being wrapped around your shoulders.

Taste chocolate ice cream.

Hear your name called from the next room.

Catch a whiff of a perfume you recognize.

Hear someone squeak a fingernail across a blackboard.

Smell something burning.

See a skyrocket.

Pick up with both hands a carton you think is full of tissue paper and find that it is filled with books.

Smell rain.

Hear snow fall.

5. List at least twelve other reactions from your own experiences and practice re-creating them.

6. Search your memory for the first experience in your life that you remember vividly. Try to recall as many details of the incident as you possibly can. Try to recall your physical and emotional reactions.

7. List and describe briefly six other situations from your own experiences in which you can recall how you felt. Imagine your way through the experience again and see if you feel some of the same emotional reaction that you did originally. Concentrate on each step that led to your emotional response, making use of the sense memories, body positions, and movements involved.

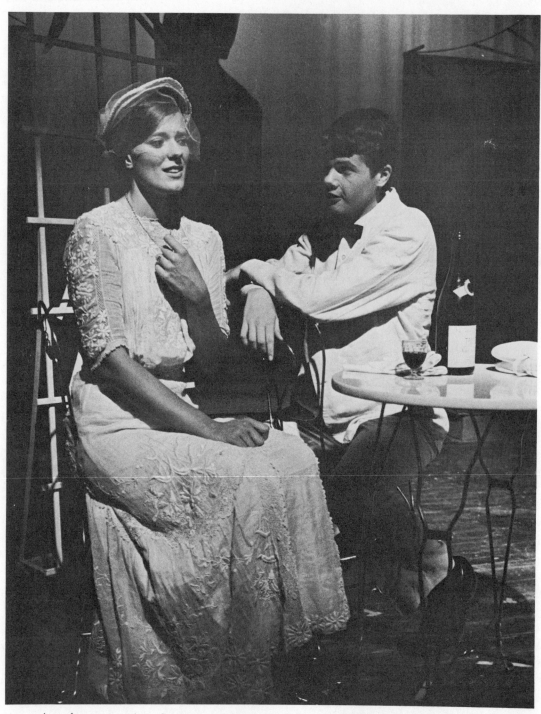

A tender moment from Summer and Smoke *by Tennessee Williams, as staged at Webster Groves High School, Webster Groves, Mo. Ernestine Smizer directed.*

Chapter VI

IMPROVISATION

We come now to the next step, and a big one, encompassing the various forms of improvisation, theatre games, or any of a number of other terms all based on spontaneous, unrehearsed acting out of an idea or situation.

The term "improvisation" should not be confused with "pantomime" or "charade." Charades and "The Game" are usually team competitions in which an individual tries to use pantomimic movements and signals that will enable his team to guess a specific activity (charades) or a specific sequence of words such as a book title or song title (The Game). The person doing the acting-out cannot use words.

The word "pantomime," though once used to designate what we now generally call "improvisation," has come to mean mainly a detailed presentation of observable physical traits and actions. It is always without sound, and can be carefully planned and rehearsed. The pantomime remains largely objective. Improvisation, on the other hand, is not planned. Its form springs spontaneously from the subjective approach of the actor, and it has numerous forms—both spoken and wordless.

For instance, you might do a *pantomime* of an old man sitting down on a park bench, taking an apple out of his pocket, and eating it. To do this you would be concerned with presenting as detailed a representation as possible of both the major movements and the smaller bits of activity, which in the terminology of the theatre are called "business." Crossing to the park bench and sitting are *movements;* taking the apple out of the pocket and eating it is *business.*

On the other hand, you could do an *improvisation* on a weary, embittered old man sitting down on a park bench and being offered an apple by a child. Here you would concentrate on what happens to you, what you feel, and what you finally do, and the movement and business would grow out of these.

The dictionary definition of the word "improvise" says, "To simultaneously compose and perform . . . on the spur of the moment." In theatre history you will find early recorded forms of the use of improvisation, probably the most notable being the improvised street comedy of the Italian Renaissance theatre, known as Commedia dell'Arte. In this form the actors started with a basic plot or scenario, were assigned certain characters to play (each of which had well-defined personality traits and plot functions) and literally made up the play as they went along.

In your own experience and observation you have been introduced to improvisation in the rainy-day play of children. A favorite form of indoor entertainment is playing school, assigning someone to be the teacher, the naughty child, the teacher's pet, etc., or pretending that the doll has a broken leg and assigning a mother, a father, a nurse, and a doctor to act out the situation.

Before considering the improvisation that is simultaneous performing and composing of words, let's think about some that are wordless.

One frequently used means for starting the limbering up and freeing process that is one of the aims of improvisation is the adoption of animal traits or machine characteristics while performing in a human situation.

Suppose you were to imagine yourself entering a banquet room and crossing to take your seat at table as a person with the characteristics of each of the following animals. First think them through, picturing the type of movement you associate with the animal and the particular character traits you think the movement indicates:

1. a friendly puppy
2. a whipped puppy
3. a fox
4. an elephant
5. a squirrel
6. a basset hound
7. a cat
8. a lion

After you have given each of them a try, perform the basic situation again, this time including a nonverbal acknowledgment of the person seated on each side of you. That is, a smile, a quick nod, a surreptitious "sizing-up" or whatever you feel the animal traits of your character would dictate.

Try the same situation with these machines as the image for the character traits of a person:

1. an adding machine
2. a decrepit automobile
3. a windmill
4. a "whisper-jet" airplane
5. a pneumatic drill
6. a sports car

You might even see what happens if you use:

1. an eggbeater
2. a piece of purple velvet
3. a wet paper towel
4. a powder puff

Now let's move into more extended forms of the individual nonspeaking improvisation. As a trial run for the ones in the work assignments and the ones you will devise for yourself, try this situation:

You are a student, and your assignment for a class tomorrow morning is to read 100 pages in the textbook. You have already read about half of it. You are tired of reading, and besides you're thirsty. Decide to go out to the kitchen for a Coke, get as far as the door, then wonder if you should take the time. What time is it? Check the amount you have left to read. Calculate mentally how long it will take you to do the rest of it, based on how long it has taken to get this far. Decide on a course of action, and do it.

This is not a true example of improvisational form, since you have been given detailed suggestions of the kind of thing one *might* do if the improvisation had merely stated, "You are a student with a 100-page reading assignment due tomorrow morning." To complete this detailed example, your decision might be not only to go for the Coke, but to chuck the whole assignment. You might decide you must finish the reading now, and set about doing it, or perhaps you'll give yourself a goal—ten more pages, then you'll go.

If possible, do even the individual nonspeaking improvisations with another person watching you, or better still, in a group. After each of you presents his improvisation there should be discussion. Each viewer should relate exactly what he got from the scene, and the actor should see how this tallies with what he thought he was conveying, or meant to convey. Pinpoint the areas that did not come through clearly, and try to determine why. Each step of the action must spring from a definite and recognizable motivation, and the transitions from one step in the action to the next should be as clear as they would be if you handed out typewritten sheets explaining what you are doing and why you are doing it.

Nonverbal improvisations with another person are an excellent intermediate step to verbal improvisation. If you return to the student situation and this time add the presence of a roommate, *inter*action between two people occurs. Each person would be pursuing an independent course of action, but it would be modified and changed by the presence of another person and what he is doing. If your activity is based on finishing the required reading, and your roommate is applying fingernail polish, or doing push-ups, or practicing the guitar, see what happens.

The improvisation in which you work with one or more people and add the final major element—*voice*—is the one to be studied next. The essence of the spoken improvisation lies in its being spontaneous and remaining spontaneous. Its aim is not for the actor to become simply glib and gabby.

As a people, Americans might be accused of being afraid of silence. Students do their homework with a transistor radio plugged into one ear or the television set on full blast. Supermarkets, elevators, beauty shops, restaurants all throb with background music to aid in avoiding silence or even the possibility of just a quiet hum of activity. The move to introduce recorded music in subways and buses in New York City was narrowly defeated by a laudable group who considered compulsory music listening an invasion of privacy. Silence for more than a few seconds on the radio or TV makes us think something has gone wrong

with the set. A delay of any kind in a broadcast obliges the announcer or newscaster to keep on saying *something,* even if it is numbingly repetitious. We can't have silence. And probably the oldest contributor of all to the anti-silence idea is the motion-picture industry. In the typical "lavish" production, if you were cast ashore with a stranger on a desert island and had a scene of mounting tension and little dialogue, you two would have that 100-piece orchestra there with you and all those violins getting more and more shrill to fill the pauses and *prove* that tension exists. As an actor on stage in the same scene, you and your fellow actor would have to *play* those pauses.

In improvisation, don't be afraid of silence. A vacuum is one thing; silence is another. Silence that is filled with listening, reacting, feeling, and finally erupts into speech because it is *needed*—this is your aim in spoken improvisation.

The duo and multiple character improvisations in the work assignments are suggestions. You and your partner or the group with whom you are working should create scenes to be improvised. Start with situations that are well within your range of experience and be careful not to include too much. Oftentimes suggested improvisations read something like this: "A young married couple, bitterly estranged, meet in the waiting room of the emergency unit of the hospital. They are waiting for a report on their small daughter, who has been hit by a truck. The nurse enters and tells them the child will live, but will be blind. The husband rushes to comfort his estranged wife and drops dead as the nurse faints." You can see what an acute spasm of bad acting that could precipitate.

Start with bare essentials—a statement of the situation, its setting, and who is involved. Work conscientiously, within the structure of the situation you have set up, so that you avoid letting the whole thing dissolve into a free-wheeling romp or a shouting match with nothing actually being accomplished. Remember that you have a lot of listening to do. Be aware of both the verbal and nonverbal communications you are getting from others. Is some person saying one thing, and quite clearly indicating by other means something quite different? Don't preplan what you will say. It must be constantly adapted to spring from what the other actors are doing and saying. Try to be aware of every possible nuance in the entire situation and above all, speak only when you want to or when the situation compels you to. Your behavior between the words, within the words, and under the words is what you are seeking to develop. This creativeness can keep the playing of a part fresh and true, while remaining strictly within the dialogue written by the playwright and the movement and business devised by the director and the actor.

Most professional acting classes depend in large measure on the various forms of improvisation for training novice actors. Great excitement and joy result when, in the course of a session, someone gets so angry that he really socks his partner, or when someone actually bursts into tears. Occasionally the sock on the jaw is the result of a personal grudge, and the tears an outcome of frustration induced by premeditated heckling on the part of the instructor. But they are *real*. You can't hit somebody by figuring that maybe you ought to, and you can't fake freshets of sopping-wet tears. Equally and perhaps more important, however, is that you seek to explore situations that demand your finding the truth in lesser emotions, and these sometimes demand harder work and greater concentration. You won't have to fly into a rage or burst into tears nearly as often as you will need to illuminate and make true more subtle relationships between human beings.

A rather prevalent tendency for the beginning actor is to fall into playing attitudes of either sarcasm or boredom, both of which are negative and extremely chancy. The use of these attitudes is easy because they afford a general cover-up for other emotions that would leave the actor more vulnerable, or in which he might lose face or look foolish. There's a certain feeling of superiority in the aloofness of sarcasm and the detachment of boredom, but I urge you to avoid them. The actor must be vulnerable, he must bare his soul and feelings through his character, and the very purpose of improvisation—to free the actor of inhibitions and false, façade-like reaction—is defeated if he takes refuge in cover-up attitudes.

From the standpoint of audience response, too, they are dangerous. The heart of the theatre, the unseen pulse that makes it live, is the empathic response of the individual watching the performance. It is feeling *with* the character rather than *for* him. When misfortune befalls him our response is not to feel sorry for him, but to feel his sorrow as our own. When he is victorious, we don't just think it's nice that things turned out well for him, we experience *his* exhilaration. This empathic response is not controllable by anything or anyone. It will not occur because you wish it to, nor can it be bidden to leave. Bertolt Brecht is said to have desired his plays to bring forth judgments and decision rather than emotional response, but if you see a superb performance of *Galileo* I defy you not to be moved to laughter and to tears. The very last attitude you would want to inspire in the individuals watching your play would be one of detachment and boredom.

Another whole area of improvisation is used for two very specific problems that may occur in a play during rehearsals or during its run. I am not talking here of the Broadway "long run" in which the actor may be playing the same role six nights a week and two matinees for a year or more. Many times amateur groups and schools schedule performances for a series of weekends rather than a consecutive run of four or five nights. When this plan is used, a brushup rehearsal is called, usually the day before or the afternoon of resuming performances. If some scenes seem to have gone stale, or to have lost their life and vigor, the director may employ several types of improvisation to bring new insights and restore the freshness of the playing. Sometimes these are used in conjunction with the final week of rehearsals, when the whole thing may seem to have gone flat. A brief description of improvisations used for these problems is given in Chapter XI.

What we are concerned with now is use of improvisation to help you and the other players get at the reality of a scene that has proven especially difficult, or one in which you haven't been able even to begin to find your way. This can happen if there is a wide gulf between what the characters are saying and the true values that must come out in the scene. Or sometimes the life and times and the actual situation your character is in may be so remote from your own that you need a basis for associating the two.

It can be an exciting experience to get at these problems through improvisation, but one essential must be scrupulously observed. The situation and characters you decide to improvise must have the *same basic motivations* as those you are trying to unravel. Let me illustrate.

A few years ago I saw a demonstration of this technique applied to the scene in Shaw's *Saint Joan* in which the Maid is trying to persuade the weak and spineless Dauphin that he must assume his place as king and allow her to lead the army. Two students read through the scene from scripts, but they had been working on it for some time, so it was more than a reading. They discussed with the director the problems they were having with the relationships in the scene, and he assigned the following improvisation: The girl was to be a young, unknown actress who has read the first play of a timid, insecure young writer. The pro-

ducers are negotiating with a known star for the lead part because it is a great role. The girl is to try to persuade the playwright that he must insist she be given the part.

What developed from this was a shallow personality conflict, with the girl becoming louder and more insistent, praising her own talents, and the playwright finding very little to say and clearly wishing by any means possible to get rid of her. It ended in a draw. Since they had started with character motivations that had practically no relation to those in the Shaw scene, the improvisation could not go in the right direction to help them. When they again played the Shaw scene, carryovers from the improvisation produced disastrous results. Joan became blatant and self-centered, and the Dauphin was battered into insensitivity rather than inspired to action. At no point, however, did the director suggest that the improvisation was not a success.

Be on guard against thinking everything and anything that happens in improvisations is great; lots of them just bog down and cannot be brought to any conclusion, as this one did. The occasional one that really takes off and produces something stimulating more than makes up for all the ones that don't work. You can learn from the fizzles, too, so long as you *know* they're fizzles.

For this improvisation to have a chance of working, the girl must be seeking to do something or get something that is not for her personal glory. Perhaps she is a student trying to persuade the drama teacher to present a play she has written. The play deals with a highly controversial school issue in terms of student attitude, and the teacher agrees that the views she has expressed need to be heard. However, he is new in the job, and is afraid that presenting it may bring down a storm of criticism from several sources. From an improvisation along these lines, the two students might have been able to work through to a conclusion in which the girl does indeed succeed in persuading the teacher to do the play. From this, there could be elements and experience that would help to illuminate the Shaw scene.

SUMMARY, AT THIS POINT

Mathematics is sometimes referred to as an "instrumental" science. There may be a few mathematical geniuses for whom solving arithmetic problems is an end in itself. But mainly mathematics is used to accomplish something else—to calculate the energy generated by Niagara Falls, to build a bridge, to fly to the moon.

So it is with sense memory, emotion recall, and the many uses of improvisation as related to finally playing the play. They are invaluable means of enlarging awareness, adding resources, and unleashing reserves of imagination you didn't even dream you had. Study them. Use them. But remember they are instrumental and not ends in themselves.

The aim of improvisations is to work toward freeing the actor from the rigidity of copied, memorized, cliché reactions and help lead him into the realms of creativity.

No formula says the use of such and such improvisational methods will positively produce creativity. This step of your training is highly individual in its applications, and its degree of effectiveness displays the same breadth. I'm sure successful actors may be found today who have never improvised a single scene, but I would surmise that many, many more have gone through the often painful first steps of improvisation that lead to increased physical, verbal, and psychological freedom and at last contribute to genuine creativity.

In a world in which we are all fighting to preserve our identity as individuals in the face of steadily mounting influences that threaten to make us disappear into impersonal classifications, acting remains an individual creation. It comes into being, however, only through interacting with other individuals, both real and imagined.

Train yourself to be acutely perceptive. Strive to take in not only information about people and things, but also to capture emotion. Register the nonverbal communications that tell you more about a person than the words he is saying. Feel what it must be like to be that ailing person, painfully making his way along the sidewalk. Photograph in your memory that look on your friend's face when he is unexpectedly drenched by a high-spurting drinking fountain.

Sensitivity to the individuals, the situations, the emotions around you contributes the largest treasure your acting fund can have. But much, much more important, this kind of awareness deepens and enlarges your capacity for appreciation, joy, and compassion as a human being.

WORK ASSIGNMENTS

Improvisations

Nonverbal

1. You have not had anything to eat for two days. At some distance you see a table filled with food. Approach the table and find that it is only a mirage.
2. You are seated comfortably in an easy chair. From a distance you can hear a dance band playing a waltz. Your body responds to the music. Finally rise and move in rhythm with the music you are hearing.
3. Do the same situation, but this time make it a rock group.
4. It's a gray day. You are cramming for an exam. Last time you looked out the window it was raining. You get up to stretch, walk over to the window—and it's snowing.
5. You are seated on a platform as one of a number of people to receive a prize. As a succession of glowing introduc-

tions are made, each time you think the name at the end will be yours. Finally it is.

6. You are strolling along the street on a pleasant day. You see a figure approaching on roller skates. As it gets near, you see that it is a fully dressed chimp. He skates on by you, and turns the corner.

7. You come out of a store and start walking in the opposite direction from the one you meant to. You are due at an appointment in a very few minutes. Be aware of someone standing in a doorway observing you as you have to reverse your direction.

8. You are reading a fascinating book. You become aware of small sounds that you can't identify at first. Decide that it sounds like a mouse scratching around in the wastebasket. It is.

9. Unwrap a long-awaited gift from a wealthy relative who always sends either something really fabulous or just a token trinket.

10. Working with a partner, do the nonverbal improvisation on page 57. Repeat it, using several different sets of independent activities, still keeping it nonverbal.

Verbal

1. With the same basic situation, you and your roommate are both trying hard to concentrate on the particular study you are doing. Comments and bits of conversation finally lead to abandoning study.

2. Teen-age offspring approaches parent to get use of the new car. Reverse roles and do it again.

3. You and your sister (or brother) are visiting in a large city for the first time. When you return from a sightseeing trip you find that your room has been ransacked.

4. You and a partner enter from opposite ends of your playing area. You are friends who have not seen each other for many years—first you pass without recognizing each other, then each realizes he knows the other.

5. In a group of at least six people, improvise the following situation: In scorching heat you have been pursued by enemies intent on destroying you. You have eluded them and are entering a cool cave. After a time you hear sounds that may be the enemy. Will they find your hiding place?

6. Form as many groups of three people as your numbers permit. Each group is to discuss and decide on a situation, and the identity of each person. Present the improvisations in turn, taking time after each one to analyze what action, feeling, and characters the viewers got from the playing. Compare this with the overall intent and the individual intent of each person in the improvisation. Try to be as specific as possible in the discussions, pinpointing particular moves, attitudes, and lines that contributed to the impressions received.

7. On the second round have each group do an improvisation given them by one of the other groups. Again evaluate effectiveness.

A tense scene from the Hallmark Hall of Fame production of Bernard Shaw's Saint Joan. *The director was George Schaefer.*

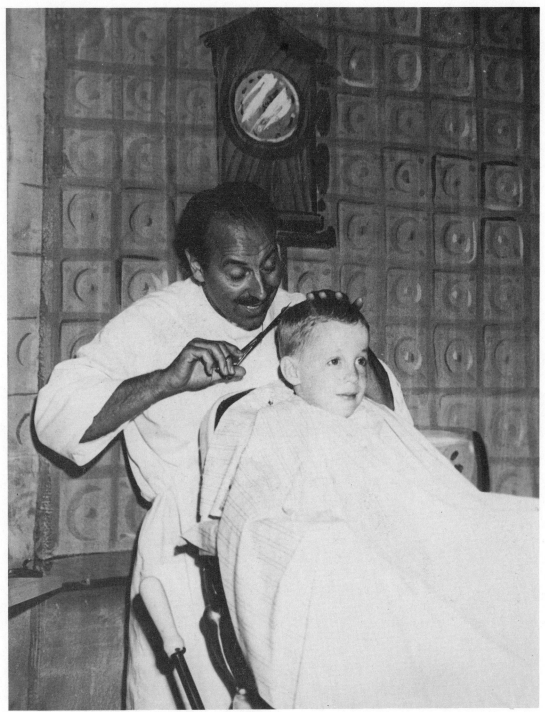

Comic Strip *by George Panetta, directed by the author, Ruth Rawson, won the Obie Award for the best Off-Broadway play of the season.*

Chapter VII

TRYOUTS AND AUDITIONS

Often when a school or community production is announced there isn't time to get a copy of the script to read, or it may be available only in hard cover or a collection you don't want to buy. We'll assume you are trying out for a play you know little or nothing about and discuss some techniques of reading for tryouts that may increase your chances of getting a part. Then we'll pick up again with work on the script you are using for your acting study.

To facilitate the readings usually several copies of the script are on hand so that you may at least glance through the descriptions of characters and see which ones might be right for you. You may also find that the director and committee holding the auditions do not see you at all the way you see yourself and will ask you to read for a part you had not considered. Be prepared and willing to read for anything. When an actor says, "Oh, I wouldn't be interested in reading for *that* part," he has practically assured himself of not getting *any* part.

If I had my way, tryouts would never be held using the actual play that is to be cast. Instead scenes would be used from other plays with characters of approximately the same age level and general characteristics. Almost invariably the funniest sequences in a comedy and the highest dramatic moments in a serious play are the ones chosen for reading, and by the time the director and the acting aspirants have been through preliminary and final tryouts most of these passages have been either horribly mangled or beaten to death. But that decision is made on the other end of the line. The actor in a tryout is there to read what is asked and try to do it so that it has meaning and impact.

Rarely is an actor asked to do a "cold" reading—that is, one in which he has had no look at the material at all. Usually you are told which scene to look over and have a chance to do a little muttering to yourself while other auditions are going on.

It is important that you be clear on this point: You may give a certain kind of reading in an audition, win the role, and end up acting it with a wholly different concept than you had in reading it. I make this statement so you will be aware that doing a successful audition and acting are two separate areas. Successful auditioning depends on a certain amount of calculated vocal dexterity and conscious use of some techniques that apply whether you're trying out for Brick in *Cat on a Hot Tin Roof* or *Hamlet*. Successful *acting* requires a very special creativity for each part you act—it is never twice the same.

If you are given a particular scene to look over, read it quickly but carefully and decide what your character is *doing* in the scene—what's happening to him. You should verbalize this so that you say, "In this scene I am trying to sell my idea to the other character," or "In this scene I am actually defending myself as if I were on trial," or "I am trying to find out what is behind the mask this girl is wearing as she is talking to me." That becomes the center of your concentration, your behavior, and it should be clearly focused on a single activity. Nothing comes off worse than a reading that tries to touch all bases and suggest any one of six different attitudes or actions. It ends up projecting nothing. It's better to come on strong with the wrong behavior goal than to come on with a shapeless generality. At least the director and committee will see that things happen when you're up there.

If you have time and are allowed to make light pencil marks on the script, plan and mark your pauses. There's a challenge in being asked to read something we're not very familiar with that seems to say, "Here, I doubt if you can sight-read this," and the natural reaction is, "I'll show you I *can* sight-read this, and I can do it *fast*." Racing through the material proves just one thing— that you are insecure. Actually, almost everyone can sight-read fairly rapidly; it takes courage and security and self-confidence to make use of pauses and give meaning to the reading—so mark them. In the thousands of auditions I've heard by both professionals and amateurs I can recall only a few cases in which the pauses were overextended and the rate of reading too slow, as compared with countless instances in which the reading was rushed and meaningless. Remember, we are all disfluent in varying degrees at various times. When you are just talking conversationally you don't have the entire wording for what you are going to say worked out in advance. You pause, you search for words; often you repeat a word as you seek to phrase your thoughts. This should be your *planned* technique in giving a reading, to avoid a steady stream of words pouring forth at an unchanging rate as though someone had turned on a faucet. If the playwright has given clues to

the meaning he wants by indicating important words in italics, be sure to give them the additional stress he has asked for.

If you are given a choice of sitting or standing, stand. Even though you may think your knees are shaking to a degree that must be noticeable to everyone, you will have a better-supported voice and appear to have more strength and presence when standing. It's a stronger body position, and it makes you feel stronger.

Do manage an occasional look at the person reading with you, and if he has a long speech, take the opportunity to really listen attentively even if it's a stage manager whose reading makes Johnny One-Note sound as if he sang at the Met. But never *never* make eye contact with the director, any member of the audition committee, or anyone other than the person reading with you. If you are reading alone, you may fix on a point slightly above the heads of the group listening to you and address that point if the scene is with one other person, or a variety of focal points if you are supposed to be speaking to several people. Emphatically, however, do not look at those who are auditioning you, once you have begun the dialogue.

Listen carefully for any ideas they may offer about qualities they are looking for in the character, and do your best to translate them into behavioral terms for what your character is doing. Suppose, for instance, you are given a few generalities such as "she's a very warm, friendly person" and "she's enthusiastic and energetic." These suggestions would mold the *way* in which your character goes about his action, and will affect what your character hopes to trigger as action or reaction from the other person.

If there is something in the passage that you don't understand or a name you don't know how to pronounce—ask. If you try to ignore a passage you don't understand on the theory that it will just sort of blend in, your theory is wrong. Hearing a name mispronounced produces a feeling in the listener somewhat akin to the bodily sensation you get if you step into an elevator expecting it to go up, and it goes down instead. The same thing is true for all mispronunciations. Failure to use the correct one can be highly detrimental to the effectiveness of both reading and conversation, so make a good, up-to-date dictionary one of your close companions.

The correlation between the amount of time you spend sight-reading aloud and your facility in being able to sight-read effectively is almost a perfect parallel. The more hours you pile up in sight-reading practice, the greater your confidence and ability will be. But be sure to use actual dialogue from plays for this purpose. Excellent collections of plays are available in paperbacks, and you can accomplish two things at once: First, you will widen your knowledge of theatrical literature and second, you will gain facility in sight-reading.

Needless to say, I am not talking about reading the plays silently. If you still have the idea that there is something spooky or a little nutty about speaking aloud when you are alone, there is no better time to rid yourself of that faulty notion than right now. And I don't mean just mouthing the words, or speaking sotto voce—I mean using good, full, projected voice.

It is nearly always a shock to the members of the cast when they begin rehearsing in the actual theatre or auditorium that will be used in presenting the play, and the results can be rather devastating. Unless the ability to project and focus the voice has been mastered, you may find that you are incapable of being heard without feeling that you are shouting. If you must become preoccupied with employing a totally different vocal technique from the one you've used as you created your character—if your character does not now sound at all the way he did in other, smaller settings—you may have a lot of extra work to do getting a balance of truth in your playing to go with the necessary vocal projection.

A final word on the importance of your coming to tryouts and first rehearsals with a voice trained to do what you want it to—both in projection and inflection: Directors cannot and will not double as vocal coaches. That is not their function. Given a choice between two actors, each of whom would bring interesting qualities to a part, the direction of the nod is often determined by which one has the better projection.

For practice in sight-reading it is a good idea to read aloud one entire scene or segment of action, then choose a character and reread it, doing only the character's lines aloud and reading the others' silently. When you can work with a partner or with a group, so much the better, but you *can* practice alone, and ten minutes of sight-reading dialogue should be added to your daily work routine.

Mary O'Connell directed this production of Bertolt Brecht's Mother Courage *at St. John's University, New York, N.Y.*

Mary O'Connell directed Bernard Shaw's Pygmalion *at St. John's University in New York City.*

A scene from The Second Shepherd's Play, *produced by the University of Redlands, Redlands, Calif., under the direction of Albert and Bertha Johnson.*

Chapter VIII

BEGINNING TO SEARCH
FOR THE CHARACTER

Thus far in the Work Assignments you have been asked to read your play twice—once for the plot and characters, and your first reactions to them; a second time to be aware of the symbols and abbreviations used for movement in the play. Now it is time to read it again, not yet in terms of your character, but in terms of the structure of the play.

Pay particular attention to the steps in the action, and at the end of each sequence that has notably advanced either the plot or the revelation of character, stop and say aloud what has happened. At the end of each act, or of the whole play if you are using a one-acter, summarize verbally these steps of action, making clear which ones represent a climax or turning point in the conflict. Determine which action represents the *ultimate* climax of the play, and what the following steps are that lead to the conclusion. This assignment is much easier said than done, but it is imperative that you have a solid groundwork in knowledge of the whole play's structure or your character cannot function as he should. Take time to do this part of the study thoughtfully and precisely.

If you are to appear in a production of the play you are studying, your director will undoubtedly call the cast together before the start of actual rehearsals, and you will discuss the play together. You will make note of the points just mentioned, and arrive at an overall approach to the play to embrace individual character concepts and the values sought by the director. This is a vital step, and it does not mean that the cast will be playing with sameness, but rather will be striving for the utmost in individual characterization consistent with a cohesive concept of the play as a whole.

This depth of knowledge concerning the play will be put to practical use as you progress in developing your character. One of the criteria you will constantly apply is: "Does the action I am playing in this sequence grow out of what has gone before, and is it true in terms of what is to follow?" Many a seemingly brilliant idea for a certain small segment of action has had to be thrown out when judged as part of the total action. The plot may be full of surprises, characters may reveal facets the audience had not dreamed of, but these cannot be unrelated moments of virtuosity played for an isolated effect. Unless they are an integral part of the whole, they become false cues that mislead the audience and destroy the truth of the play.

In the pre-rehearsal study of your character you might think of yourself as a fisherman, casting out a huge net to draw in every bit of information, thought, emotion, imagination, that could possibly apply to the person you are playing. You will keep the character "loose"—fluid and flexible—all during the period of development. Early rehearsals are a period for searching and trying out.

Where is the logical place to begin the search for your character? Within the words of the playwright, of course. So now we come to the fourth reading of the script, this time in terms of your particular character. Note as a start the physical description of your character, but don't take this too literally. You were probably cast, or chose for your study, a character that you as an individual resemble sufficiently in general appearance to be acceptable. So-called "type casting" always exists to some degree, but if the author has been extremely specific and described your character as "tall, dark, intense, with eyes that are much too large for the face," the description has an applied rather than explicit value. You could look just like that, and not be able to act your way out of a paper bag. Of much more importance is your being able to play "tall, dark, intense, and big-eyed."

Plays based on historical characters offer a different problem. In *Lawyer Lincoln* we need to have a tall man who can be made up to look as much like Lincoln as possible, since everyone is well acquainted with the details of his appearance. This becomes a vital part of the consideration in casting. But unless the character is of such magnitude that he falls into this same category (Grant, Lee, Franklin D. Roosevelt are some other examples), the physical resemblance is not nearly so crucial a factor and sometimes need not be considered at all. Judge Davis in *Lawyer Lincoln* is also based on an actual person in history, but it would be safe to assume that few in the audience would have any idea what he should look like. The most important thing will be to play the character's *being* as he is presented by the authors, even though the physical appearance of the actor may not match the playwright's description.

Descriptive words abound in the directions for movement and reactions in most scripts, giving valuable clues to indicate how the playwright sees your character. Make a list of such directions as "with authority," "vehemently," "he rushes to the door," "irked." Do you see how such a character would contrast with one whose list began with "tentatively," "softly," "she moves hesitantly toward the door," "alarmed"? But be careful not to jump to conclusions and set up a rigid, cliché character on the basis of the first evidence you find. You are searching.

At the same time you are reading the play to list the directions that reveal character, make note of things said *to* you by other people that reveal their appraisal of your personality and behavior. These might be such lines as "You don't try to understand how he feels," "You're always falling in love," "I've never seen you when you seemed unhappy." But again remember, the fact that someone sees a certain trait in you doesn't necessarily mean it is there. It may be a clue to your character, or perhaps more accurately a clue to your relationship with the particular person who speaks the line.

The third list to make from this reading will be what is said *about* you by other characters. These might be such lines as "She's always late," "She thinks she's better than everyone else," "He never thinks of his own gain." You should tabulate also who it is that says the line, and to whom it is addressed.

Finally, you will be working from the beginning to find out what the words of your own character say about him. What do the things he *does* tell you? What do you know about his background? What can you surmise?

Rereading the play cover to cover is at once one of the most surprising and most valuable parts of your preparation and should be continued at intervals all through the rehearsal period. As your character grows individually and in relation to other people in a situation, new insights into the play open up. Oftentimes another reading of the whole script, even after you think you've squeeezd everything from it, may reveal something so simple and so right that you will wonder how you could have overlooked it.

Chapter IX

THE EARLY REHEARSALS

You know from your study so far that quite explicit directions for movement are usually given in the play script; however, many directors choose not to follow these exactly as given. Sometimes the setting has been considerably altered to meet the limitations of a particular stage, and the movements are no longer workable. Often the director and the actor arrive at quite different moves based on the particular interpretation of a character or of the play as a whole. The ways in which directors work are as various as the combinations of methods used by actors. Unless the play consists mainly of two- and three-character scenes that allow the actors to move about pretty much as they choose, your director probably will wish to block the major movements in the first rehearsals. These should be written into your script in pencil as the rehearsal proceeds—written, so that you can duplicate the moves accurately the next time through, and in pencil because many changes in movement will be made as the play takes shape.

During these early rehearsals you will be sizing up the other characters, listening to them, and getting to know them. Keep your attitude about them and your own character alert and open, and work like a demon. These rehearsals and the time you spend in addition to called rehearsals are the "perspiration" that Thomas Edison said makes up 99 percent of genius. In acting, doing the 99 percent to the fullest extent of your abilities helps insure that elusive 1 percent of inspiration needed to make your playing light up and shine.

From the very first rehearsal, whenever you have been called to be there, but are not onstage, observe the rehearsal from out front. Try to determine what your director is striving for and evaluate honestly the progress you can see in development of values and characters. If the nature of the rehearsal is such that you gain more by going over lines and scenes with other available actors, do that, being sure you've told the stage manager where you will be so you can be called for entrances. There is never enough time in rehearsals, so make the best possible use of every minute offstage as well as onstage.

Before considering the characterization in depth, let's dispose of some of the other necessary nuts and bolts in the construction, which will be needed as rehearsals proceed.

Your director will give you a deadline for "books out of hand," and it is important that you meet this. To that end, here are some rigid "do's" and "don'ts" and several more flexible suggestions.

1. Memorize verbatim.

If you find a wording that is especially difficult or that seems insurmountably awkward for you, talk it over with your director and arrive at a cut or change, if necessary, but do not memorize approximately or by "getting the idea" across in your own words. This is one of the rigid rules, and it has a threefold reason back of it.

(a) Suppose on a particular page of the script there were four characters with lines to speak and each of them made four changes in wording. These might be putting "well" before a line, substituting a word of similar meaning for the one in the script, linking two sentences with an "and," or any one of a number of other seemingly minor alterations. But sixteen "minor" alterations per page can ruin the structure and style the playwright labored to create. No one would think of letting Romeo say, "Soft, what light breaks through yonder window," and every playwright and every script deserves the same respect.

(b) Unless you memorize verbatim you can never *know* that you know your lines. Suppose you have settled into wordings that you use most of the time, then you go back to the script for one of the periodical re-readings of the play and to brush up on your memorization. If you find dozens of variations between what you've been saying and what the script says, you are in deep trouble. Nobody's got a copy of that script you've been improvising and paraphrasing all over the place. You now have to unlearn the inaccurate lines and memorize the words as written, because all of your cognitive and creative concentration must be free to go into acting, not remembering. Your memorization must finally be so solid that you can forget it—if you know what I mean.

(c) If you are not accurate with your lines and cues, your fellow actors should, and probably will, pounce on you. That exhaustive, all-important listening cannot be accomplished by actors wondering what and when the cue will be, or even if.

2. *Don't try to go without your book too soon.*

This is almost always directly linked with the inaccurate memorization just discussed.

Also, it is unfair to slow the rehearsal pace by needing prompting every other line.

3. *Experiment with these tried and true aids to memorization.*

(a) Do not try to memorize any unit less than one complete act of a full-length play or the entire script of a one-acter. Specifically, read aloud every line you have in the whole act and continue to study in this manner until you are ready to try out your memorization by having someone cue you. If you find that you are still very insecure, return to the process of reading aloud every line you have in the act. *Don't* rework a few pages at a time, going over and over them until you have them by rote, and then move on to the next few pages. It is usually hard to convince beginning actors that this "whole" method of memorization works, but sound principles of learning underlie it. The thought sequence assists you in learning the word sequence—you are memorizing the flow of action as well as the lines. It's even better if you can do this for the whole play, but, although the total time invested would probably be less than you will put in to learn it an act at a time, it requires longer study periods, which are often hard for the amateur actor to fit in with his other activities. In addition, the most common practice is to require books out of hand a single act at a time, even though this often results in the final act's needing extra work just before dress rehearsals because it has had the least time spent on it.

(b) Do your line study aloud and in full voice whenever possible. This way you get a triple-powered sense impact—you see the words, you hear the words, and you feel the articulating of the words kinesthetically. They all reinforce one another to speed up memorizing.

(c) If you have a tape machine, record the entire speeches of all the other actors in your scenes, leaving out only yours. Play the tape, listening, shut it off when it's your cue, say your line, start it again, etc. Don't record *only* the cues. Surely by now we all know why. The sight of an actor jolted out of his mental tune-out by the last three words of a speech and suddenly leaping into action is the inevitable consequence of learning only cues. *You must listen to everything.*

(d) Read through all the lines in the act you are memorizing just before you turn off the light at night. Your subconscious will put in some good licks at the memorizing while you sleep.

(e) For passages or lines that trip you every time, figure out some kind of memory device (mnemonic) to use until you get them nailed down. This usually takes the form of an association, the wilder the better, that you make from the cue to your opening words, if that's the problem, or within the segments of a passage if the whole thing is troublesome. Look at this passage from *Angel Street* by Patrick Hamilton, and consider the problem it is for Mrs. Manningham to have these wordings *exactly* right, so the tension builds as the playwright planned and the entire concentration of the actress stays with the action:

INSPECTOR ROUGH. Ah yes, but in this case there is something more than morbid compulsion—there is real treasure there to be unearthed if only he can search again, search methodically, without fear of interruption, without causing suspicion. And how would he do that? *(All at once she rises.)* Don't you think—What's the matter, Mrs. Manningham?

MRS. MANNINGHAM. *(As she looks at gaslight brackets and backs away to RC.)* Quiet! Be quiet! He has come back! Look at the light! It is going down! *(Pause as the light sinks.)* Wait! There! *(Pause.)* He has come back, you see. *(As she looks up at ceiling.)* He is upstairs now.

Here's one series of devices one might use to lock up this sequence. Since this is the first of several passages concerned with the dimming of the gaslight, one could probably

remember "Quiet! Be quiet!" without too much trouble, but associating the opening with Queen Bee could be used. The next three exclamations could be built around the word "hell." *HE* is the beginning of the first phrase, the next one starts with *L,* and the last one has to do with *GOING DOWN.* This is followed by William Tell (Wait! There!). Now the focus shifts from the lights to the Inspector as she tells him again what has happened, personalizing it with "you see." This is followed by United Nations (he is Upstairs Now).

These may not be associations that would work for you; figuring out mnemonics is a highly individual matter, but it is the basic device used in all systems of memory training. See what you can do with this sequence:

INSPECTOR ROUGH. Not if we are clever enough. And this one here doesn't even ask for cleverness.—You see, Mrs. Manningham, there are all manner of—*(Light comes up.)*

MRS. MANNINGHAM. Stop—stop talking—Haven't you noticed? Haven't you noticed something?

ROUGH. Noticed? I've only—

MRS. MANNINGHAM. Stop! Yes—I was right. Look. Can't you see? The light! It's going up. He's coming back.

ROUGH. The light?

MRS. MANNINGHAM. Quiet! *(Pause, after which the light slowly goes up in a tense silence. Whispering.)* There. It's come back. You see. You must go. Don't you see? He's coming back—He's coming back and you must go!!

That one is really a challenge, but see how quickly you can form a pattern that steers you into an absolutely verbatim memorization. If you think of these lines again in a week or two or a month or two or even longer, the chances are you will still be able to say them with complete accuracy.

Although the small tape recorder is excellent for studying and correcting diction errors and is a useful tool in memorization, it cannot be used to much advantage in studying other aspects of acting. The low, intimate manner used when speaking into a hand mike bears little resemblance to the projection needed in speech for the stage, and interactions with other characters must be present to have an acting situation. When you listen to recordings of plays it is often very clear that the script was not being acted, but merely read into microphones.

In the superb recording of *Death of a Salesman* with Mildred Dunnock, Lee J. Cobb, and other members of the original Broadway cast, an actual set and an elaborate system of microphones were used, so the play was being acted as it was recorded, and the effect is brilliant. Recordings made during a public performance are rarely of good quality because microphones can't be hung all over the stage in public view. It is, however, an excellent way to study the pace and timing of the show, especially in comedy.

A video-tape machine is available in the audio-visual lab of many high schools and colleges, and the opportunity to record and photograph simultaneously, then replay, can be very helpful in the study of a scene. Some actors, however, experience so much additional tension at the thought of being filmed that the performance projects none of the qualities of the stage portrayal. Continued use helps to overcome this tension and increase the effectiveness of video-tape study.

When rehearsals have reached the point for scripts out of hand, don't fall into the habit of doing silly things if you need a prompt. Stamping your foot or snapping your fingers or groaning or pounding your forehead with your fist won't help you remember the line the next time. It may make

you feel more comfortable because in essence you've said, "Gee, am I dumb!" thereby beating anyone else to the line. But memorization, verbatim memorization, is difficult and no one springs into rehearsal word-perfect at the end of a week or two. The point is to make use of the prompt by really registering it and letting it sink into your mind without distractions.

In performance there is no such thing as an unnoticeable prompt, either from the stage manager or another actor in the scene. Most directors instruct the person holding book to be loud and clear if a prompt is needed. Better one fast dealing with the illusion-shattering impact of a forgotten line than three or four whispered endeavors that the actor cannot hear although everyone else can, including the audience. The substitute for depending on prompting is the developing of ensemble playing based on knowledge of the whole play, which enables the company to pull themselves out of line jams. If you have done your preparation well, and are listening as you should, you will be able to come to the subtle rescue of any actor in your scene who may get into difficulty and you can just hope that he has prepared as well as you have and can throw you a life preserver if you need it.

One last suggestion. As the rehearsal period progresses you should assume responsibility for using substitute items for any hand props you will be using in the play, and do the same for any articles of costume such as hat, purse, gloves, coat that you will be handling. The director will ask the prop crew to have the exact items there for all of the dress rehearsals, but the sooner you can incorporate the business into the rehearsal (in other words, as soon as you no longer need to carry your book), the better. If the costumes are out of the usual range that you're used to wearing—for instance in a period play with knee breeches for the men and huge hoop skirts for the women, start wearing something that is as close an approximation as possible to what you will be wearing in the play. All the things mentioned in this chapter are vital mechanics of the acting process. They must be dealt with methodically and thoroughly so they serve as aids, not hindrances, in the creative process of developing your character.

Scene from the Amateur Comedy Club production of Visit to a Small Planet *by Gore Vidal in New York City. Ruth Rawson was the director.*

Ruth Rawson directed this staging of Herman Wouk's The Caine Mutiny Court-Martial *by the Amateur Comedy Club of New York.*

Chapter X

DEVELOPING THE CHARACTER

You often hear it said that an actor must "get inside his character." The mental image that brings to me is of someone stepping into a hollow suit of armor and then issuing forth as if to say, "Look, I have become this character. I have disappeared inside the visible form that is he."

It is far better to let the character get inside you. You are the instrument that is going to give him flesh and blood and thought and feeling. You can't disappear, and no actor can actually become the character he is playing. Although it is considered high praise to say of an actor, "He didn't *play* so and so, he *was* so and so," the actor knows this is ridiculous.

Take a good strong flashlight and look at the lighted bulb through the clear glass lens. Now cup your fingers over it so the light shines through your hand. The original light is still there, but the warmth and glow of life are added. Wiggle your fingers and you manipulate the light into changing forms and shadows. So it is with acting. The source of the light you are to transmit belongs to the playwright and the character he has written for you, but it is this light shining through you that creates the character and gives it the breath of life. Only you, the actor, can do that.

All arts are bound together by common principles of selecting, simplifying, and arranging details into a meaningful form capable of eliciting an emotional response from the receiver. It is an involvement—the receiver shares the emotion the artist feels in creating the work. It is an experience—quite beyond casual enjoyment or being merely entertained. It is as true of painting, sculpture, and architecture as it is of the performing arts of music, dance, pantomime, and drama—and it is timeless. It is what makes you look at a painting and breathe, "That's great!" Or feel stirred by music, or shaken by a drama, or exhilarated by a ballet. It happens when the artist has felt an emotion and believed it with such totality himself that you also believe, and the emotion is infused in you. Great painters, sculptors, and architects use tangible elements of paint, metal, marble, and glass to house the feeling. The notes and patterns and words of the performing arts are transformed into feeling through the tangible elements of design and through the unique intangible contribution of the individual human being.

There is a world of difference between being lifelike and having reality. Sometimes the actor becomes preoccupied with making the character lifelike and gets so bogged down with fussy details and trappings that he fails to find the heart of his character. It can mean the difference between a good "performance" and a really great job of acting. Neither one is easy.

In your early weeks of study you have been working on the techniques that go into acting—training and tuning the instruments of voice and body to do what you ask them to, sharpening your awareness of both perceptual and emotional information, working to free yourself from inhibitions that block creativity. If your early search has been done well, you will be asking yourself not what more you can add, but what you can discard. Creating the true character now becomes a process of stripping away irrelevant detail; simplifying and clarifying to reveal what has reality.

The actor in school and community plays is often faced with the problem of playing a character many years older than himself—sometimes even to the extent of two generations removed. In developing an old-age character such as Grandpa Vanderhof in *You Can't Take It With You,* you will need to put to expert use the observations you have done on movement. Here you will need to use the postures and body positions typical of age to lead you into a *feeling* of age, but be sure they are accurate and truthful. Many times beginning actors overestimate the infirmities of age and begin doddering about and speaking with a quavery voice when playing anyone over the age of 60. When the sources for the creation of an "age" feeling come from within, it is not necessary to *do* anything startling to your voice. The rate will probably be slower, the voice more hesitant and not so resonant, but these qualities should grow out of what you are doing rather than being imposed from the outside. Then they are convincing, and the creation becomes an old-age character, not a caricature.

Playing in highly stylized period plays and in Shakespeare makes some special demands in voice and movement beyond those required for the typical "realistic" production. Readings on these problems are given in an annotated bibliography at the end of this book, since a more thorough-going discussion is needed than can be given here. The basic approach to the character, however, remains the same.

Briefly, as regards playing dialect parts, it is best to concentrate on the rhythm and pitch pattern of the dialect rather than too many specific pronunciations. Dialects should be suggested, so the lines can still be easily understood and there are not wild variations in the degree of dialect among the cast members. Here again, recordings can be of immense assistance.

Acting is, of course, *inter*acting. Your character cannot live in isolation; he exists only by means of his relationships with other characters in the play and his reactions to the events making up the action. You cannot "play" the character you have now described and found except through the conflicts, sympathies, changes that occur in him and to him. The depth and reality of your acting depends on the *degree of receptiveness* that you are able to maintain in terms of the way your character thinks, feels, and acts. You are getting to know him very well; he is inside you, and the responses you make come from him.

The quality called "presence" or sometimes known as "taking stage" is probably best explained as a feeling of such confidence radiating from a performer that it commands an audience to center its attention on him. It is not confined to acting. The stand-up comic, a preacher in the pulpit, a circus acrobat, a vocal soloist all exhibit some degree of "presence." Although some are born with a greater potential for this quality than others, it is generally developed through experience. The experienced actor would be expected to have more confidence than the beginner, so although you can't develop more confidence simply by deciding to, you are probably aware of the fact that this quality has been growing as you progressed in your study. It will continue to develop as you gain experience.

One very dangerous phenomenon is called "duality," and the slightest glimpse of it by the audience can totally destroy the believability of a character.

Let me try to explain this as clearly as possible, for it is the most vital area of the whole listening and acting endeavor. Of course the actor *is* someone pretending to be someone else, but the spectator must see only a single image wherein every move, word, thought, and reaction comes only from the character being played. If, for any reason, the actor loses his immersion in the character's subjectivity and projects a comment on *himself* as the character he is playing, the character no longer exists. We no longer believe.

This phenomenon is not confined to beginners; it is in fact often evident in some of the biggest "stars" of stage and screen, but it marks the difference between a *performer* and an *actor*. This revelation of duality sometimes takes the form of a kind of self-appreciation—a segment of the actor projecting an unspoken but unmistakable "My, I am great!" or "I really am adorable doing this," or "I am indeed a funny fellow." But it is not always this. Anything at all that reveals the actor's awareness of his own being as *separate* from that of the character will wipe out the believability of the character.

You may have seen actors "break up" on stage—that is, laugh *as themselves* at something another actor does. Or you may have seen television comedy shows in which the star gets a big laugh by commenting, as himself, on something that is happening in the play. These are sometimes carefully rehearsed as part of the show, especially if the script is weak and needs all the bolstering the star personality can give it. Audiences eat it up because it proves to them that the star is just an ordinary human being like themselves. I am not saying that the "per-

sonality" star displaying his own virtuosity while pretending a character is not enjoyable. It can be a dazzling display, but it is not acting. It is performing.

In the beginning actor, this glimpse of duality most often stems from the actor's retaining a self-consciousness about what he is doing. One segment of him may be projecting a defensive "Look, *I* know this is silly," or an apologetic "I know I'm not very good," while the rest of him is saying the lines and going through the motions of the part. This leaves the actor totally without power, since his attitude toward *himself* is self-deprecatory, and the character he was playing has disappeared. It is such an actor whom someone described by saying, "He might as well phone in his lines."

There is no safety net for you, the beginning actor, and there never will be. You must present your character completely, and with faith.

About half way through the rehearsal period is a good time to get out those first notes you made about the play and about the characters. The objectivity of those first reactions is sometimes a good balance for the subjectivity you now have, particularly about your own character. You may find some refreshing and usable insights. Try to find extra time to get together with other members of the cast with whom you share scenes. See what you can discover that might add new facets or greater depth to the relationships. Are you really listening and playing to other actors by using what you can get from them as well as what you give to them? Try improvisations. When you think you have found something good in a particular scene, examine it in terms of its truth in the whole play. If it seems to fit, try it in rehearsal and see what happens. If it works—if it feels right to you and does what the director wants done in the scene— keep it.

By the time you move into the final week of rehearsals the hours and energy you have spent fulfilling your responsibilities in creating a part will be merging with the joy and exhilaration of playing it. Even if you were never ever to appear in a public performance of a play, but simply to work on scenes and reading performances with others who have a similar interest, the study of acting will have given you something that nothing else in the world could give. You'll see.

Dickens' A Christmas Carol *was presented at the A. L. Brown High School in Kannapolis, N. C. Mrs. Janie Yates directed.*

Chapter XI

YOU AND YOUR DIRECTOR

It has been said many times that the American theatre is a director's theatre and if it's possible to gather all the myriad varieties of directing under just one general heading, this is probably true.

In those sessions before rehearsals start, when the cast and director talk through the values, characters, and approach to the play, most directors listen carefully and make use of cast feelings and ideas in making decisions. As you rehearse he has been assessing what each actor brings to the part, and sometimes this is quite different from what he had expected on the basis of your tryout. As you have been growing in your characterization the director may be shifting and sharpening the emphasis in various ways to make the most effective use of you in terms of the ensemble. This ensemble quality in the performance of a cast is hard to define; it is the quality that, through group cohesiveness, enhances the individual.

That may sound somewhat paradoxical, but its principle might be stated in the old cliché that a chain is no stronger than its weakest link. Old-fashioned "stars" used to require (and often insure by absorbing nearly the entire salary budget) that no other actor in the cast be anything more than just barely adequate—the theory being that brilliance from any other source would diminish that of the star. Today's theatrical criteria demand that each part be cast and played at the highest level possible; the interplaying of such a group produces a strongly woven and vivid fabric, not a haphazard accumulation of threads.

In judging individual and ensemble effectiveness, final decision must rest with your director. Usually if something feels right to you it will be right, but not always. The actor must be ready to experiment not only with his own ideas, but with anything the director asks him to try, and the final responsibility of finding the "why" of a particular action or move is always up to the actor. Much of the time the movement is dictated by the action in the scene, but occasionally you may be given a direction you find difficult to justify. If after real digging to find a truthful motivation you can't come up with a satisfactory one, then it is time to discuss the move with the director.

If theatre appears to have developed more definite "don'ts" than it has "do's" it is because the job of seeing what is wrong is infinitely easier than seeing how one goes about getting something right. An actor may play in many ways to accomplish the value needed, but the value is quite particular. The actor must believe in his director and trust his judgment.

It follows that the actor must not listen to anyone except himself and the director. I don't mean that there should be no give and take other than the dialogue of the play between actors. Far from it. Actors should question and discuss what each is getting from the other in a scene, but the decisive word is the director's. "Suggestions" from actors who are not in the scene, and above all "advice" from a friend, relative, or loved one who may have been allowed to see a rehearsal, must fall upon totally deaf ears.

At some point in the rehearsal schedule —when all the freshness seems to have gone out of the script and you are wondering why in the world you ever thought you wanted to act—your director may call for a period of improvisation. He might ask you to switch parts with someone else and improvise the scene from that character's viewpoint, or even ask you to convey the meaning and feeling of a scene by using the abc's or nonsense syllables in place of the dialogue. These are all valuable means of shaking up the players and adding fresh insights.

For at least the final week before performance you will be doing complete runthroughs, and the director will present notes he has taken during these performance-like rehearsals. These suggestions and corrections should be carefully noted and applied, and I urge you not to be dismayed if the list is long. When the performance has reached a point of excellence, then it is possible to polish and refine it; a scarcity of notes unfortunately may mean that there's just not much use.

These notes are usually given before the entire cast rather than individually since many of the suggestions affect a whole situation and involve more than one actor. Some think this method is hard on the actor's ego, but notes that should be given in private can be given in private and there is much to be gained by the whole company's being aware of the desired changes.

Once the moves, pacing, and emotional structure of the play have been set, the actor must not make major changes. Of course this does not mean the play is to settle into carbon copies—it can't, if the actors are doing their hyper-listening. No doubt some performances will be more inspired, or in some intangible way better, than others; that is the potential that adds the excitement that only a "live" performance can produce. But every director has his own little collection of horror stories about an actor in the midst of performance making a radical change of move, or playing a totally unexpected wayout reaction. Sometimes the play never does get back on its feet after one of these. The departing director's remark to the cast after opening night that he would be back in a week to take out the "improvements" is all too often justified. Neither should any prop be added or business changed or costume altered without the consent of the director.

Romeo, in the production of Romeo and Juliet *staged at the Brighton High School, Rochester, N. Y. Paule Knoke, director.*

Chapter XII

JUST BEFORE THE CURTAIN
GOES UP

As surely as a mechanic is going to get his hands dirty when he fixes your car, you are going to get stage fright when you act. Just why the stage should get blamed for a tension that can also afflict a student in a classroom, a guest at a banquet, the bridegroom at a wedding, and countless others, I'm not quite sure. It all has to do, in some way, with being the object of focused public scrutiny, and it is incurable. Happily, like many other afflictions, it can be arrested and controlled, and can even make a positive contribution.

Certainly no one believes any longer that "a bad dress rehearsal means a good opening night." It may seem good by comparison, if what preceded it was a shambles. But before opening night you should have been through at least three complete dress rehearsals, probably with a small invited audience on the last one, so even if this is your first acting assignment you will have some of the feel of playing before an audience.

An important "never" must be observed between actor and audience and it is this: The actor never makes eye contact with any member of the audience, except under very special circumstances that we will discuss presently. Your point of focus, though you may be facing directly front, is never one that allows you to actually see any one person and this is true whether you are speaking or silent. Sometimes beginning actors think no one will be aware of just one quick glance, but if even the farthest upstage member of the chorus actually looks to see if Row C, seat 5, has the expected occupant it's as if a bell rang and a flashing sign said "Tilt."

One exception in straight plays is when speeches, by the playwright's intent, are directed to the audience. Sabina does this in *The Skin of Our Teeth*; the Stage Manager in *Our Town*; Tom in *The Glass Menagerie*. "Asides" to the audience are often indicated in old melodramas, and sometimes in period plays and in Shakespeare the audience is directly enlisted to sympathize with the plight of a character or is given plot information by direct word. This kind of communication does not include the soliliquy, which, though the actor may be alone on stage, is a self-conversation or thinking aloud and is not audience-focused. Musicals, both in proscenium and arena staging, present some notable exceptions to the rule, and they are discussed in later chapters.

The hours you and your fellow actors have spent perfecting the memorization and getting to know the whole play are the greatest insurance available against experiencing acute stage fright. Theatre annals are filled with stories of actors ad libbing a scene several minutes long while a frantic stage manager rushed to the dressing room for an actor who had forgotten an entrance. I have seen an actor go back and carefully pick his way into the correct scene when another actor, listening only to cues, made a mistake and suddenly catapulted them into the final scene of the play.

Additional steps in preparation are to be taken just before curtain time. If your stage manager has given you a one-hour call, that is, to be at the theatre one hour before curtain time, it is up to you to decide if that is sufficient time for you to get into costume and makeup and be ready to go on.

Being ready means that you will have personally checked to be sure any hand props you use are in their proper place onstage or are on the prop table at the correct entrance if you are to bring them on. You will walk through your first entrance, and get the feel of the set by moving around through the various areas. If there are pieces of furniture that were unavailable for rehearsal and are new to you, walk around them, sit in them, sense them. If any furniture is not placed exactly as it has been in rehearsal, ask the stage manager to come and check it. In doing these things you are removing as many causes for anxiety as pos-sible, and you are preparing psychologically and kinesthetically to play your part.

Before the stage manager calls "Places for act one!" the rest of your preparation should be whatever suits you. Actors are as individual in their pre-performance warmup as they are in their acting, but the good performer does prepare in some way before going on just as a singer vocalizes and a dancer limbers up with exercise. Some actors go off in a corner and brood; some prefer to be quietly chatty and friendly in the dressing room; some go through elaborate creating of what their character is doing just before he enters the scene. If you go in heavily for this latter means, don't get so involved in preparing that you fail to hear your cue, or do in-place running for a breathless entrance to the point that you get onstage and can't say anything. It has happened.

Precurtain tension makes a positive contribution by heightening your energy and sharpening the sensitivity you need to give a good performance. Once you make your entrance the concentration you've been centering on yourself and how you feel goes into the concentration of total listening and attending to what is happening on stage. You no longer have room for stage fright.

Chapter XIII

PLAYING IN THE ROUND

I've never talked with anyone who feels neutral about playing in the arena theatre; it seems to elicit either great enthusiasm or total rejection. Many actors still refuse to play in this kind of setting because they demand the protection of that "aesthetic distance" that the proscenium theatre gives. Other actors feel that the proscenium actually becomes a barrier, and welcome the increased audience participation afforded by the round.

The first known form of theatre was the huge outdoor amphitheatre in which presentations of the Greek tragedies and comedies were staged. Its form was either circular or oval, with a central acting area and row upon row of raised tiers capable of seating thousands of people. This is the fundamental design of the arena theatre. Later, the Greek form became a three-sided or partial circle, and this in turn served as the fundamental design of the Elizabethan and present-day "thrust" stage.

We are considering now the small theatre, or even just a room, which can be converted into an arena stage simply by placing two or three rows of chairs around four sides of an oval or rectangular area left clear for acting. The tent or gymnasium seating 1,000 to 3,000 or more is quite a different matter and will be discussed in the chapter on playing in musicals.

Probably the greatest argument in favor of playing in the round is an economic one.

Naturally when the necessity for a complete stage set is removed, and the merest skeleton pieces may be used to induce an audience to conjure up a garden or a ballroom or a kitchen, one has eased not only the monetary burden but also the hours of time and talent needed for designing, building, painting, and erecting a set. Being relieved of these burdens allows the school or amateur group to offer many more productions and provide acting opportunities for many more individuals. This is the primary reason I am such a staunch defender of the use of this form of production, though I think its effectiveness varies widely with the particular script being used. The thrust stage, discussed in the next chapter, manages to combine many of the best features of proscenium and arena staging.

Great amazement was caused by this "true" experience in arena playing, reported from many sources several years ago: An actress crossed to a table placed near the edge of the acting area and picked up a cigarette as part of the rehearsed business of the scene, whereupon a playgoer in the front row, without a moment's hesitation and without disturbing the scene, lighted it for her. It is somewhat doubtful if this happened quite as often as reported, but it was indicative, at that time, of the possibility for far greater intimacy in the audience-actor relationship than that afforded by proscenium playing. It might be considered one

95

of the gentle and circumspect forebears of today's wildly improvisational "Happenings" and all-out audience-participation movements in the theatre.

Whether or not the cigarette-lighting story is apocryphal, the actor playing in the round does come upon both advantages and disadvantages in having the audience in his lap. I believe it is in some ways more difficult than playing in proscenium and demands greater effort to retain concentration, though it is less demanding vocally. It might be compared with the motion picture close-up because even the slightest move or smile or frown registers with great impact on those seated only a few feet away from you. Since no one in the audience sees the *whole* picture, as everyone in the proscenium theatre does, meticulous care is needed to keep the central audience focus where it should be, and not allow numerous little "side shows" to distract their attention.

Unlike the big arenas, which have a sort of moat or neutral zone around the acting area (one section of which is the orchestra pit), the edges of the acting area in the small arena are undefined by anything other than the legs and feet of the front-row occupants. You may really have to watch where you're going if you get a couple of first-class sprawlers.

Movement in general is greater in arena playing, for the obvious reason that sufficient variety must be employed to keep audience segments from all four directions engaged visually. This rules out the playing of any scene, especially duo scenes, very long in one position, and brings up one of the aspects that make arena playing difficult. You, the actor, will be called upon to justify and motivate movements that your director may give you largely for the sake of changing the stage picture and composition. All too often arena playing takes on the look of the "one, two, three, hup" of the football line when the actors shift position merely to be visible to another part of the audience. Here is a situation in which the creativity

you are developing is needed to help you sustain a continuous flow of suitable motivation.

For many years the most over-used business in the theatre was lighting a cigarette. Notice I said "lighting," not "smoking," because most of the time the actor could not possibly continue to handle the actual business of smoking, for the length of time required to make it realistic, without strangling as he combined it with the process of speaking. As a result the effect was that of a stage full of nervous people frantically lighting cigarettes and then putting them out for no reason at all in the nearest ash tray. Use smoking as business only when demanded by the script. It is both messy and precarious—lighters don't work, matches break, cigarettes continue to smolder if the prop crew has forgotten to put water in the ash trays.

The term "motivation" does not mean you always have to *do* something. It is not necessary to actually get the handkerchief out of the purse you've left on the table, or to pick up and look at a photograph on a bookcase across the room. But your character must have an intent in his moves, even if it is merely that he wishes to be closer to or farther away from another character because of a relationship inherent in the scene. If on any move at all (and this is true in any sort of playing) someone were to ask you, "Why did you do that?" your reply should never have to be, "Because the director told me to." You must make the moves belong to your character, even though they may have originated as somewhat arbitrary necessities.

Another major difference in playing in the round, along with the increase of movement and small business, lies in the manner in which actors are positioned for duo or shared scenes. Instead of facing each other directly as they would in proscenium playing —that is, in such a manner that they would collide if either moved forward—for the arena they are on close parallel tracks rather than a single one. With this positioning, if either moved forward, he would brush the other actor's shoulder, but he could pass. They will still look at each other to play the scene, but while two sides of the audience are seeing the scene in profile, a third side will see the face of one of the actors and the fourth will see the face of the other. Unless this kind of positioning is maintained, two segments of the audience are stuck with a view of an actor's back.

Finally, the directions given you either in the book or by your director must be adapted to the fact that there is no longer an "above" and "below" or an "upstage" and "downstage." Places for entrances and exits are designated by number, and usually all four of the corner aisles are used. Directions are given largely in relation to other characters and the furniture, such as "cross to Jim's right and exit at #1" or "move to the left of the sofa," with right and left in this case, as always, being that of the actor involved in the move.

In the previous discussion about prompting and its difficulties, the reference was mainly to proscenium stage. In arena style all the same difficulties prevail, only more so. Clearly, any prompting from an offstage person is impossible, and although it is occasionally possible for an actor in proscenium staging to get away with whispering a prompt to a fellow actor if he is quick about it, this could never go unnoticed in the round. Sometimes another character can simply step in and say the missing line, or if the line can come only from the particular person who is intended to say it, the assist may be in the form of a question suggesting the content of the dropped line.

When the unexpected happens in any kind of staging—if a vase of flowers tips over, or you drop something, or a picture falls off the wall, you can't just ignore it, hoping the audience will, too. Correct the situation as well as you can, just as you would if it occurred in any other setting, and get on with the scene.

Thornton Wilder's The Skin of Our Teeth *was produced by the James Monroe High School in The Bronx, N. Y., under the direction of Laurence Fineman.*

Another scene from the James Monroe High School production of The Skin of Our Teeth. *Laurence Fineman directed.*

Chapter XIV

PLAYING ON A THRUST STAGE

The variety of heights, widths, depths, and proportions of stages is tremendous, but the three major types that determine certain elements in your playing are the *proscenium,* the *arena,* and the *thrust*. Almost any playing arena that you can mention, from municipal stadium, through Broadway theatre and high-school auditorium, to a stage on the back of a truck or just a room, is a form of one of these three basic types. We've already talked at some length about proscenium and arena as they affect the actor. Now let's consider the thrust stage, which is one of the oldest and also the newest popular form of stage.

The elementary idea of the thrust stage is that the playing area has only a back wall, with the audience seated on curved tiers surrounding the other three sides. This one wall may be a permanent structure made up of pillars and archways, or it may consist of an adaptable or changeable group of flats, similar to those used in proscenium. Levels of various heights, accessible by stairways, are usually part of the permanent structure. This was the Elizabethan theatre of Shakespeare's time, probably the most notable example of which is the famous Globe Theatre, which housed most of his plays.

As the stage gradually withdrew from the audience to behind the proscenium, a sort of vestigial remnant of the thrust stage remained in an area extending a short distance in front of the curtain line toward the audi-

ence. This area, known as the apron, varied in depth from two to six or seven feet, and occasionally action was allowed to spill over onto it during the long period when footlights were standard equipment in every commercial, school, and amateur theatre. As the use of footlights waned and finally disappeared, use of the apron as a playing area largely ceased because it could not be lighted. Most school and community theatre groups found themselves equipped with on-stage general lighting, which began at the back of the set and ended abruptly at the curtain line.

Commercial theatre by this time had begun to use lighting instruments hung in full view of the audience from the balcony rail and "trees," which might be located on each side of the balcony or at each side at the very front of the orchestra. Amateur theatre, following the trend, found it could again light the apron, which thus regained its place as an area for action. Often two or three rows of seats were removed so platforms could be built to extend the apron farther into the audience area. This resulted in a definite feeling of closeness to the audience in scenes played outside the proscenium, which both spectator and performer found enjoyable. For many years, however, the convention of using a front curtain remained inviolate, and the actor was often obliged to scurry into position behind the proscenium to avoid being hit on the head by a descending curtain, or worse, find that a curtain had closed behind him, leaving him in no-man's land. When this happened, the curtain, which had clearly been in two parts, by some mysterious process became welded into one undivided whole without an opening through which the actor could escape.

The next step in the evolution to the return of the thrust stage was the discontinuing of the use of the front curtain. It was considered quite an innovation to come into a theatre or school auditorium and find the front curtain already open, revealing the set. The signal that the play was about to begin was the customary dimout of the house lights, with the actors taking their places onstage in the blackout before bringing up lights on the acting area.

Much of the pioneering in this movement to break out of the rigid bounds of proscenium theatre, which had been the only American stage form for so long, was done in college and amateur theatres. Impetus for the trend was added by the tremendous success of the beautiful Shakespeare Theatre in Stratford, Ontario, which is not a facsimile of the Globe Theatre but a modern application of its basic design. Commercial theatre in America joined in rediscovering the freedom and variety afforded by the form, and such structures as the Shakespeare Theatre in Stratford, Connecticut, the Tyrone Guthrie Theatre in Minneapolis, and the Vivian Beaumont Theatre in Lincoln Center, New York, are outstanding examples of the thrust stage.

You've probably already thought of many advantages other than increased audience involvement afforded by the thrust stage. Here are some of them:

1. An audience equal in size to one you would wish to accommodate in a proscenium house can be distributed on three sides rather than just one. No seats will be as distant from the playing area as the last rows would be in proscenium, thus improving both visual and auditory factors.

2. The cost of elaborate sets is greatly reduced, since the creation of the mise-en-scene is accomplished either entirely by set pieces and furniture in the case of the permanent structure, or by building only one wall instead of three if a more representational set is desired.

3. Entrances and exits through the audience may still be used for a variety of effects just as in arena playing, but in addition access to offstage areas is readily available without going through the audience. This makes possible quick costume changes, surprise entrances such as those needed in mystery plays and melodramas, and permits bodies to get up and out unobtrusively. This is no small point when it comes to staging something like *West Side Story* for matinees or in any situation in which a complete blackout is impossible. The entire effectiveness of the Act I ending can be ruined in arena staging if the slain leaders of the two gangs, in full view of everyone, get up and run down the exit aisles. The audience knows they aren't dead and doesn't want them to be, certainly. But the time to welcome them back as actors to the land of the living is at the curtain call, not when they are existing for us as characters in the play. I saw this problem successfully handled by a director who keyed in a scuffle among other members of the gangs in which several were knocked to the ground, identities were lost in the attention to action, and the exits accomplished without notice. Some such camouflaging is sometimes necessary in thrust staging also, but the problems are considerably lessened.

4. The use of platforms and stairways of varying heights affords great flexibility in pictorial composition and heightens the feeling of action. If one character not only pursues another across stage but also up one side of a flight of six steps and down another, there's a lot more activity and excitement. Although no law prohibits use of levels in proscenium and in arena, they are not nearly as effective. The absence of anything to back them

in the arena makes their use extremely arbitrary and stepladdery in effect. Proscenium is hampered by the fact that much of the audience is already below stage level, and adding levels increases the angle of viewing. The steeply raked tiers of the seating around the thrust stage put no one at less than level with the stage floor and the vast majority above it.

Of all the considerations, this last mentioned, affording of greater action and visual interest, is the major asset of the thrust stage. Broadway is still bound to the proscenium by the structure of its houses, though an increasing number of productions are dispensing with use of the front curtain and availing themselves of the variety and interest of entrances and exits using the aisles. But as new facilities are built for school and community groups and experiment continues with adapting auditorium and gymnasium to approximate the thrust stage, the return to this form is gaining wide popularity. I believe it is the most satisfying of all forms of stage for the actor, combining the best elements of both proscenium and arena into a distinct form with unique characteristics and potentialities.

Chapter XV

PLAYING IN MUSICALS

The arts of acting, singing, and dancing, each capable of standing individually, exist conjunctively in the presenting of musicals and revues and present special challenges to the actor. Much of the solution of these problems (assuming you have started with a proven book and score) lies with the director, but it is vitally important that you, the actor, be fully aware of what the demands are and be capable of making the best use of directing suggestions and your own resources.

In opera only a very small portion—and sometimes none—of the exposition is spoken. Musical recitatives take the place of dialogue. In the musical comedy and musical play, definite dialogue scenes of considerable length are alternated with music and dance numbers, though the extent to which music is used varies greatly. *West Side Story, Most Happy Fella,* and *Guys and Dolls* are three with somewhat more extensive scores than the average.

In the operetta form, and in most musicals predating *Oklahoma!,* the musical numbers were quite separate from the spoken parts of the production, and the often-flimsy plot came to a complete stop each time a musical number came along. In the present-day musical the intent is that music, dance, and dialogue shall all advance the plot and maintain the tempo of the whole production. Because of this approach, in both the writing and directing of musicals, the songs develop out of the action, advance the plot, and flow into the next action. This continuity must and can be kept, even though the music and dance numbers are followed by audience applause.

It is, then, the performer's responsibility to be able to pick up a spoken scene, after a loud, spirited production number that gets audience applause, with sufficient vocal and physical energy to avoid a big letdown. This is not always merely a matter of volume. The emotional intensity of a spoken scene can make it fully as dynamic as a production number, and a number of staging techniques are employed in both proscenium and arena playing to help equalize the spoken action and the musical and dancing action. Let's look first at those used in proscenium.

Because most musicals have many different scenes, but employ only one intermission, it is necessary that scene shifts be so rapid that they are accomplished without interrupting the flow of the plot. Marvelous mechanical devices are available in some commercial houses and in many high-school and college theatres. One of these is the revolving or turntable stage, which can have two or three different sets revealed by presenting a certain segment of the circle to audience view. Those that have been used can be changed during the use of another segment, thus affording an almost unlimited possibility for multiple settings. Sometimes sets are placed on platforms about half the width of the proscenium opening and seven or eight feet deep. These are called "wagons" and can be ready in the wings, to be pulled into place by cables or "walked" on by a trained and competent crew. Sometimes complete or partial changes of set are part of the action, as in the building of the teahouse in *Teahouse of the August Moon,* or are accomplished during the opening lines of a song or scene.

By far the most used device for rapid scene changes in musicals is still employment of extra curtains to serve as backdrops, dividing the stage into three separate planes. These are known by number: "one" is the downstage third of the stage, just back of the front curtain; "two" takes in the center plane plus one, thus occupying two thirds of the stage; "three" is the full stage. Most big ensemble or chorus numbers are played "in three" and the shift back to a dialogue scene is accomplished by lowering a backdrop or closing a traveler curtain so the scene is played "in one." Since this is the one third of the stage nearest the audience, it is the strongest area, and this helps minimize the change in decibel level from a stage full of singing, dancing people to two or three who are speaking.

If no scene shift is required, the dialogue scene may begin in three, but is usually brought down into one as soon as possible. On the other hand if a major full-stage shift is needed following a number in three, the apron may be utilized for a dialogue sequence. This does not mean that the front curtain is closed; an additional (usually highly decorated) drop is often hung only a few inches back of the house curtain, and this can be dropped in or pulled shut to permit the shift to go on while the action is played on the apron.

Just as in playing dialogue a character must look at the person to whom he is speaking, so in both proscenium and arena staging a song whose message is directed to another character on stage must be sung to that person. It looks pretty unconvincing if the hero

is pouring out his heart in a love song looking directly at the audience, while the heroine clings unnoticed to his arm. And at the end of definitely person-directed songs of this kind the director will devise some movement or business to occupy the actors, in character, while the invigorating waves of applause roll in. You can't acknowledge applause from the audience on a song you sang to someone else—they weren't even supposed to be there.

This brings us to a very important point about acting in musicals—the matter of actual eye contact with the audience. Whereas the sharing of a thought or confidence with the audience is, as we noted earlier, comparatively rare in straight plays, it is definitely a part of the structure and technique in a musical. Musicals are intended to bring forth a great deal more overt response from the audience than the straight play. Hence, the applause at the end of numbers does not disturb the continuity because it is an accepted convention of musical staging, whereas an actor getting a hand on an exit within an act or scene is considered a damaging interruption by many theatregoers.

The intermediate step between songs that have an onstage receiver and those sung with eye contact directly to the audience is the soliloquy song. "Maria" and "Tonight" from *West Side Story,* "If He Walked into My Life" from *Mame,* "I've Grown Accustomed to Her Face" from *My Fair Lady* are all contemplative songs that are audience-directed, but not audience-focused.

For many solo numbers, and almost all chorus and production numbers, the audience is the direct focal target. "Hello, Dolly!" becomes audience-focused when sung as a production number, "You Can't Get a Man With a Gun" from *Annie Get Your Gun,* "I'm Gonna Wash That Man Right Out of My Hair" and "There Is Nothing Like a Dame" from *South Pacific* are all direct conversation to the audience. Show-stoppers such as "Adelaide's Lament" from *Guys and Dolls* and "Hey, Look Me Over" from *Wild-*

A joyous moment in Oklahoma! *by Rodgers and Hammerstein, based on the novel,* Green Grow the Lilacs, *by Lynn Riggs. William Martin directed this revival of the ageless musical at Culver Military Academy, Culver, Ind.*

cat are powerful person-to-person appeals for audience sympathy in the first case and approbation in the second. This kind of direct appeal, done in character, is one of the musical's most potent attractions for both performer and spectator. Applause, needless to say, is acknowledged directly.

When musicals are done in the round, either in a tent or by converting a gymnasium or other large area into arena form, the rules of direction and focus for dialogue and songs is the same as in the proscenium form. The same increase in movement that was discussed regarding straight plays is true also in musicals. Musical numbers are often arbitrarily divided, the soloist playing a section of the song to one side, then turning to the other. The chorus is usually given sufficient movement so all areas of the arena have an adequate view, or if the number is done without movement, the chorus may be divided—half facing in each direction.

It is difficult to draw any generalizations about acting in musicals, since the style, size of house, and many other variables influence the playing. Let's hazard one: Generally speaking, the scale of the playing in musicals is larger than that in straight plays.

Natick High School in Natick, Mass., presented My Fair Lady, *the musical version of Bernard Shaw's* Pygmalion, *under the direction of Harry L. Garnett.*

The climactic scene in Oscar Wilde's The Importance of Being Earnest. *Staged at the Amateur Comedy Club of New York by Ruth Rawson.*

Chapter XVI

THE BEGINNING

So here we are at the end, which is really the beginning. I doubt that any actor, no matter how great, has ever thought he had reached the end of the road in learning about acting.

Perhaps one of the reasons that experience in the arts is so satisfying is that no short-cuts exist in endeavors dependent upon the creative efforts of the human individual. Man-created art, like nature's art, neither yields to nor is at the mercy of demands of expedience, speed, and pressure. The great writer still creates his masterpiece word by word, the artist stroke by stroke, the musician note by note, and the actor bit by bit.

It is my fervent hope that the material we have covered in this study will lead you to continue exploring and discovering the treasures of theatre in all its aspects—its literature, its direction, all facets of its production. And, of course, that element without which the theatre could not exist—acting.

The Man Who Married a Dumb Wife by Anatole France was produced by the Englewood School for Boys, in Englewood, N. J. Fred B. Hutchins was the director.

111

You Never Can Tell by Bernard Shaw was directed by Ruth Rawson for the New York Amateur Comedy Club.

SOURCES FOR SCENES

One man and one woman

All the Way Home	Tad Mosel
Angel Street	Patrick Hamilton
Bad Seed, The	Maxwell Anderson
Born Yesterday	Garson Kanin
Bus Stop	William Inge
Chairs, The	Eugene Ionesco
Corn Is Green, The	Emlyn Williams
Country Girl, The	Clifford Odets
Days and Nights of Beebee	
Fenstermacher, The	William Snyder
Dear Brutus	J. M. Barrie
Death of a Salesman	Arthur Miller
Delicate Balance, A	Edward Albee
Elizabeth the Queen	Maxwell Anderson
Five-Finger Exercise	Peter Shaffer
Guardsman, The	Ferenc Molnar
Hello, Out There!	William Saroyan
Hotel Universe	Philip Barry
Lesson, The	Eugene Ionesco
Long Day's Journey into Night	Eugene O'Neill
Madwoman of Chaillot, The	Jean Giraudoux
Mary, Mary	Jean Kerr
Moon for the Misbegotten, A	Eugene O'Neill
Period of Adjustment	Tennessee Williams
Picnic	William Inge
Potting Shed, The	Graham Greene
Rainmaker, The	Richard Nash
Redemption	Leo Tolstoi
Subject Was Roses, The	Frank Gilroy
Summer and Smoke	Tennessee Williams
Tiny Alice	Edward Albee
Tonight at 8:30	Noel Coward
The Astonished Heart	
Red Peppers (Cockney)	

Two for the Seesaw	William Gibson
Typists, The	Murray Schisgal
Who's Afraid of Virginia Woolf?	Edward Albee
Winterset	Maxwell Anderson

Three women

Madwoman of Chaillot, The	Jean Giraudoux

Two women and one man

Arsenic and Old Lace	Joseph Kesselring
Ethan Frome	Owen and Donald Davis

Two women

Arsenic and Old Lace	Joseph Kesselring
Bad Seed, The	Maxwell Anderson
Cavalcade	Noel Coward
Chalk Garden, The	Enid Bagnold
Children's Hour, The	Lillian Hellman
Days and Nights of Beebee Fenstermacher, The	William Snyder
Dark at the Top of the Stairs, The	William Inge
Girls in Uniform	Christine Winsole
Glass Menagerie, The	Tennessee Williams
I Remember Mama	John Van Druten
Killing of Sister George, The	Frank Marcus
Ladies in Retirement	Edward Percy and Reginald Denham
Liliom	Ferenc Molnar
Little Foxes, The	Lillian Hellman
Mary of Scotland	Maxwell Anderson
Miracle Worker, The	William Gibson
Mourning Becomes Electra	Eugene O'Neill
Old Acquaintance	John Van Druten
Old Maid, The	Zoe Akins
Separate Tables	Terance Rattigan
Taste of Honey, A	Sheilah Delaney
This Happy Breed	Noel Coward

Two men

Ah, Wilderness	Eugene O'Neill
Billy Budd	Robert Chapman and Louis Coxe
Born Yesterday	Garson Kanin
Caretaker, The	Harold Pinter
Caine Mutiny Court-Martial, The	Herman Wouk
Cat on a Hot Tin Roof	Tennessee Williams
Country Girl, The	Clifford Odets

Deadly Game, The	Friedrich Duerrenmatt
Death of a Salesman	Arthur Miller
Five-Finger Exercise	Peter Shaffer
Hotel Universe (three men)	Philip Barry
Home of the Brave	Arthur Laurents
Look Homeward, Angel	Ketti Frings
Men in White	Sidney Kingsley
Play's the Thing, The	Ferenc Molnar
Potting Shed, The	Graham Greene
Subject Was Roses, The	Frank Gilroy
This Happy Breed	Noel Coward
Thunder Rock	Robert Ardrey
Tiny Alice (opening scene)	Edward Albee
What Price Glory?	Maxwell Anderson and Laurence Stallings
Winterset	Maxwell Anderson
Zoo Story	Edward Albee

Bibliography

A selected reading list on acting and directing in period plays.

Chisman, Isabel, and Ravenhart, Esther. *Manners and Movement in Costume Plays.* Boston: Walter H. Baker Co.
Extremely explicit but rather elementary instruction in movement, dance, body positions, handling of costumes, hair styles, etc., of the medieval, Tudor, and Restoration periods, and the 18th and 19th centuries. It is concerned with externals, not touching on the "spirit" of the periods or any study of the manner in which they may be translated into present-day playing. A useful guidebook on mechanics.

Cole, Toby, and Chinoy, Helen Krich. *Actors on Acting.* New York: Crown Publishers (3rd ed.), 1957
Reading this book is a career in itself. Of great value in illuminating the history of playing classic and period plays, with applicable quotes from Plato and Aristotle on through the chronological and geographical progressions to Rome, Middle Ages, Commedia dell'Arte, etc. Little that is helpful in suggestions for present-day approach since the interviews with contemporary actors deal largely with contemporary plays.

Duerr, Edwin. *The Length and Depth of Acting.* New York: Holt, Rinehart and Winston, 1962
This is a comprehensive book, slanted toward the historical approach, and done in highly detailed fashion. Use of actual dialogue from plays is very helpful in determining present-day approach to various periods, and there is a seven-scene scenario for a Commedia performance. Excellent material on the changes in styles of acting and appraisal of current trends and tastes in theatre.

Funke, Lewis, and Booth, John E. *Actors Talk About Acting.* New York: Random House, 1961
Now available in two paperback volumes issued by Avon, these interviews have limited application to the specific problems of playing in period plays, but are thoroughly engrossing reading. Gielgud has some excellent points on style in general, and a good deal about Shakespeare in particular, as do the Lunts, who come right out and say *The Taming of the Shrew* isn't a great play and is therefore in need of tremendous imagination just to keep it going.

Golding, Alfred Siemon. *The Theory and Practice of Presentational Acting in the Serious Drama of France, England and Germany During the 18th and 19th Centuries.* Columbia University: Doctoral Study, 1962
Probably the most comprehensive and detailed work in terms of acting that you'll find. There are illustrative plates of gestures, body positions, and facial expressions that were standards for the period. The volume is entirely historical, with no material concerning translating into terms of acting these plays today.

117

Goodman, Randolph. *Drama on Stage*. New York: Holt, Rinehart and Winston, 1961

This book is made up of complete studies and backgrounds for present-day productions of *Medea, Everyman, Macbeth,* and *The Misanthrope.* Uncut scripts of all the plays and detailed comparison of original forms with translations now used are included. The book contains authoritative reviews by experts in all areas of the acting, directing, and producing of these four plays.

Guthrie, Tyrone. *In Various Directions*. New York: The MacMillan Co., 1965

A superb analysis and explanation of why the Greek plays were so great, and what prevents their being effective today as they were in their own period. The chapter on "Classical Theatre and the Entertainment Industry" is worth the price of the book. Compare his flaming descriptions of two festival performances in the theatre at Epidaurus with his comments on theatre "when the criterion of merit is how many tickets you can sell." Also there is great material on meanings, motives, and playing of Shakespeare.

Oxenford, Lyn. *Playing Period Plays*. London: J. Garnet Miller, Ltd., 1957

The four small volumes by Lyn Oxenford, who is billed as Staff Tutor, British Drama League, are a veritable do-it-yourself kit for the amateur group. She deals with the general problems of bringing present-day reality *and* theatricality to period plays, and gives very specific suggestions on acting, movement, and every aspect of the production—including costume, accessories, dance, music, gestures, hair styles, and makeup. Her explicit and authoritative manner of writing should inspire the inexperienced with at least the security of knowing they are "right" if they follow her directions. Available in paperback, the work is divided as follows:

    Part   I—Medieval and Early Tudor periods, 1066–1550

    Part II—Elizabethan, Jacobean and Stuart periods, including Masques, 1558–1649

    Part III—Restoration, Georgian and Regency periods, 1688–1820

    Part IV—Victorian and Edwardian periods, 1827–1910

Roberts, Vera Mowry. *On Stage*. New York: Harper & Row, 1962

This is the "compleat" book of information on classical and period plays. Subtitled "A History of the Theatre," it is not only that (and written in an easy, interesting style) but a most valuable reference for all areas of consideration in the producing and acting of the plays. It has a wealth of illustrations, both photographic and in diagram, lists of available scripts from each period, suggested study problems, glossary of terms—in fact, everything you want to know. A book to own.

Rockwood, Jerome. *The Craftsmen of Dionysus*. Glenview, Illinois: Scott, Foresman and Co., 1966

Chapter 7 of this book is one of the most complete, concise, and useful treatments of style you'll ever find. Illustrations and specific directions on playing medieval, Tudor, Elizabethan, Restoration, Victorian, and Edwardian periods, including information on production details.

Saint Denis, Michel. *Theatre: The Rediscovery of Style*. Great Britain: The Windmill Press, 1960

This thoroughly enjoyable volume is a printing of a series of five lectures given by Saint Denis on his first visit to the United States in 1958. His knowledge and appreciation of "style" and the French viewpoint placing Shakespeare outside the general category of classicism into its own area as dramatic poetry are but a few of the many facets of theatre covered in the lectures. I hope this quote will inspire everyone to read the book. . . . "Style is the only penetrating instrument of authentic 'realism,' whatever the period." A crystal clear definition of the difference between naturalism and realism is the basic springboard. Our current kitchen-sink drama often fulfills the former to the nth degree, but fails to come anywhere near "reality." One final quote from this remarkable book. . . . "A contemporary artist will give his interpretation of the past from the standpoint of today . . . his interpretation is bound to belong to his own country and his own time."

West, E. J. *Shaw on Theatre.* New York: Hill and Wang, 1958

In this volume there is an excellent essay on playing the "points" in Shakespeare and a searing criticism, in detail, on how Beerbohm Tree's production of *Much Ado* managed to miss them. It is entitled "The Dying Tongue of Great Elizabeth." The essay "On Cutting Shakespeare" is also of great interest in the matter of "modernizing" Shakespeare. This was written in 1919 after Shaw had allowed the cutting of his own plays for American production.

———

Helpful articles on period plays from *Educational Theatre Journal,* selected from "A Ten Year Index—1949–1958" by David Welker.

"The Nature of Mime," Graves, Russell B	May, 1958
"A Style for Shakespeare," Joseph, B. L.	October, 1955
"A Study of Audience Reaction to a Stereotype Character," Whitehill, Buell, Jr., and Kodman, Frances, Jr.	May, 1952
"Directing the Verse Play, Payne B. Iden	October, 1950
"Harley Granville-Barker and the Greek Drama," Thomas, Noel K.	December, 1955
"Recent Scholarship on the Greek Theatre," Mernodle, George R.	May, 1951
"The Language of the Theatre I: The Greeks and Romans," Trapido, Joel	October, 1949
"Teatro Olimpico, 1954," Jacobs, Elizabeth R.	October, 1954
"The Greek Chorus," Kitto, H.D.F.	March, 1956